C000017283

Memories of Colne

by

Mrs. Cryer

(Reprinted from the *Colne & Nelson Times*, 1910)

with a new introduction by

Christine Bradley

Landy Publishing
2006

© Copyright in this book is held by the author.
The terms of the Copyright, Designs & Patents Act, 1988 and the
Duration of Copyright & Rights in Performances Regulations, 1995, are
to be applied.

ISBN 1 8728 9570 0

British Library in Cataloguing Publication Data.
A catalogue record of this book is available from the British Library.

Layout by Mike Clarke. *Tel/Fax: 01282 850430*
Printed by Nayler the Printer Ltd., Accrington. *Tel: 01254 234247*

Landy Publishing have also published:

Accrington's Changing Face by Frank Watson & Bob Dobson
Oswaldtwistle Observed: Gawping at Gobbinland by Mike Booth and
Albert Wilkinson
Blackburn Tram Rides by Jim Halsall
Blackburn in Focus by Alan Duckworth & Jim Halsall
Preston in Focus by Stephen Sartin
Bolland Forest & the Hodder Valley by Greenwood & Bolton

A full list is available from:

Landy Publishing
'Acorns' 3 Staining Rise, Staining, Blackpool, FY3 0BU
Tel/Fax: 01253 895678
e-mail: bobdobson@amserve.co.uk

Introduction

When I was approached by Mr Bob Dobson of *Landy Publishing* and asked which book written on the history of Come I would recommend for reprinting, I had no hesitation in suggesting Mrs Cryer's *Memories of Colne*. Originally published in the *Colne & Nelson Times* in 1910, it is still a popular book and asked for in the library today. Being an incomer from Yorkshire and not knowing very much about Colne, when I first became Reference Librarian at Colne Library this was one of the first books I was recommended to read to familiarise myself with Colne.

Mrs Cryer's *Memories of Colne* is a wonderful, evocative social history book and a worthwhile tool for anyone doing family or local history in Colne. As you wander through Colne with Mrs Cryer, you can visualise her next to you gossiping about all her friends and relatives. Re-reading the book as I write this foreword, I was amazed at how much detail she has put into the book.

Beginning at the bottom end of Colne, just by the *Crown Hotel*, Mrs Cryer gives us a vision of a town set in rolling fields; at this time Albert Road was known as Westgate, a narrow exit from the town which was later to become known as Manchester Road and then Albert Road.

As she progresses up the road she would have had fields either side of her until she reached the Parsonage and the old Colne Hall, which in 1851 had some fifty people living in a collection of old buildings, including Jude Baldwin's beershop.

Past the church and up to Ivegate and Windy Bank and along to the top of Skipton road, naming all the shops and their trades as she passes, her memory was remarkable in remembering each trader from clogger to German barm dealer, shoe shops, high class tailors, silk hat manufacturer's, confectioner's, painters and decorators.

But it is not just a list of people, she tells a short story about each and everyone, what they are wearing, who they were related to with nicknames such as '*The Swell Hatter*', '*Dick of Ancocks*'. Colne seems to have been a very lively social town, dancing at the *Swan Hotel*, the *New Red Lion* and 'Public Day' balls attended by local gentry arriving in carriages. Her description of crinolines and the troubles ladies had controlling them and her dismay of the new clinging fashions of the 1900s is wonderful. In fact she is very observant of the fashion of the time, how fashionable gentlemen did not wear caps preferring long hair, caps being reserved for pigeon fliers, dog fanciers and prize fighters. Hairstyles also come in for some criticism a chignon being called an abomination, young ladies with fringes were treated with ridicule and their hairstyles called 'donkey fringes' and men with short hair were known as crop-eared and probably just out of prison! From the main streets of Colne Mrs Cryer takes us down Colne Lane to Waterside, where she gives us a lovely description of the Rushbearing festivities almost pastoral in their telling.

She talks of knowing the wealthy Pickles family and Sir William Pickles Hartley along with Robert Shaw of *Song of Sunrise* fame. We then walk down Windy Bank and passing more fields head up to Langroyd Hall, where Mrs Cryer was a housemaid as a young woman.

Mrs Cryer's recollections portray Colne as a small but bustling town where everyone knows everyone, and the church was a pivotal focus in the town's events. Birth, marriage and death were solemnly observed her eloquent description of the funeral of a young girl being escorted by her companions dressed in white described as 'the Church that had seen so many happy brides, carrying with us the bride of death'.

With the re-publication of this book, I hope everyone will take the same amount of pleasure I have in these gentle reminiscences of a lady who had a great love for Colne and the people who lived here in the 1850s.

Christine Bradley
Assistant Reference Librarian
Colne Library

Colne Parish Church from a sketch by W H Hey of Nelson.

MR. WM. BRITCLIFFE,

Practical Optician,

After a long and varied experience of

SIGHT-TESTING, FITTING, &c.,

in Burnley and surrounding districts, desires to thank his customers for their continuous patronage and support. Mr. WM. BRITCLIFFE is noted for the reliability of his Goods and Moderation of Prices, combined with thorough efficiency in SIGHT-TESTING, FRAME FITTING, etc. A Trial Order will be esteemed, and your enquiries receive immediate personal attention.

Lantern Lectures

Are arranged for Schools, Improvement Societies, Clubs, etc. (Any Subject.) State needs — quotation given return post.

ALL LANTERN REQUISITES
kept in stock.

NOTE ADDRESSES:

18, QUEEN VICTORIA ROAD, and MARKET HALL, BURNLEY.

Old Church Street, Colne.

MEMORIES
OF COLNE

By

MRS. CRYER, of Burnley

(Formerly Miss MARGARET JANE WARD,
of Colne),

In Collaboration with

MR. WILLIE BELL, of Burnley

(Formerly of Colne)

Reprinted from the " Colne & Nelson Times,"
March—August, 1910.

MRS. CRYER.

Albert Road, the start of Mrs Cryer's journey through Colne, with the Crown Hotel on the left, with the sign for Barrowford Road.

MEMORIES OF COLNE
SIXTY YEARS AGO.

CHAPTER I.

Oh, how intense, how vivid, are the memories of
youth! I see thee, Colne, stand out before my mind's
eye, clear and radiant in the morning sun. Oh, those
long summer days, and the slumberous summer nights.
The spell of the past is upon me. I hear the shutters
rattling against the shop windows, and voices, long since
hushed and still—the cheery voices of the friends of my
youth—are ringing in my ears. Old faces smile, and
vague misty forms come out of the darkness, and I live
the past again. I see the white moonlight on the
ancient church, and the shadows of the tombs on the
velvet sward around. There, near the gates stand a
young man and a girl. How low and earnest his voice
is; there is a light in her eyes as she listens, the light
that never was on land or sea. Ah me; it is the old,
old story, as old as the hills, and yet ever new. But
the voice that whispered that story is long since hushed
and still, and the girl to whom that story was told is
now writing these memories.

I was born at Walk Mill House on the 6th of
December, 1841, and I have had a long life
and a hard one. Trouble and reverses have
come to me, as they do to all God's children,
but I have seen His hand in it all, and, although I
am not abundantly endowed with this world's goods,
God has given me health and strength—two things
which are more to be prized than rubies. Who that

passes that busy hive of industry, Walk Mill, to-day, can have any idea of the scene of sylvan beauty Walk Mill House presented sixty years ago? It was a large square house, with a flower garden in front, where roses threw their white blossoms over the wall, and peeped through the white wooden railings leading up to the front door, also painted white. And right in the centre, but too high for us children to reach, was a lion's face, painted black, for a knocker. The white windows seemed to be so bright in the summer sunshine. Then there was a large kitchen garden that ran down to the river wall, filled with fruit trees and with currant and gooseberry bushes bordering the walk. There, in what was then a scene of beauty and peace, I dreamed the first few years of my youth away.

One of the best known educational establishments of that day was Mrs. Blackburn's boarding and day school for young ladies. It stood in Keighley Road, opposite the old toll bar and near where the Commercial Hotel now stands, then kept by Mrs. Strickland. Nearly all the best people sent their daughters to Mrs. Blackburn's School. Mrs. Blackburn herself – a stately dame, in rustling black silk, and with her hair arranged in loops over her ears, and wearing long, black ear-rings, after the fashion of Queen Victoria – used to sail into the schoolroom punctually at nine in the morning, and, standing near her desk, she would say: "Good morning, ladies," and we would rise, and, after a curtsey, say, "Good morning, Mrs. Blackburn." Then the lessons would begin. Do they teach Scripture lessons in the schools to-day? Not much, I fear. They did then, and, in my opinion, boys and girls grew up better men and women for it. A Mr. Marine came to teach music on a Wednesday, and a Mr. Tallon taught French on Thursday; and there was a lady who came from Burnley to teach us wax flower-making. We paid a guinea a quarter, French, music, and flower-making, of course, being extras. I never saw Mr. Blackburn. It was whispered that he had been a ne'er-do-well, and had left her. Then, like so many more brave women, she took up the reins of life, and succeeded. She had her mother living with her, and kept a neat, clean woman

Guy Syke: extensions to the railway sidings in 1901 led to the filling-in of the old road to Barrowford, off which ran this row of cottages. They were attached to an old fulling mill.

Demolition of Old Colne Hall, where Mrs Cryer grew up. It became the site of Baldwin's beer shop, and is now part of Albert Road.

John Wilkinson's shop, Market Street, c1900. Local historian Wilfred Spencer was born in the room flanked by the Sunlight Soap advert. The property had been owned by his grandfather, Robert Spencer. Pictured left to right are Alex Cook, Jim Briggs, Mrs Abraham Knight and Greave Shaw, with J.W. Peplow behind.

servant, named Betsy, who made splendid mint sauce for, every now and again, a favoured few, I amongst the number. She would give a tiny spoonful; just to taste, you know.

Amongst my school friends at Mrs. Blackburn's were the two Misses Midgley, from Trawden, and Miss Mary Midgley, from Carry Lane Head; a Miss Bolton, who lived next door to the school; the two Misses Hartley, from Laneshawbridge; Miss Esther Phœbe Hodgson, whose father was incumbent of Christ Church; Miss Matilda Sagar, of Heyroyd House; the two Misses Thompson, from Swanfield; Miss Ann Hartley, and her cousin, Miss Holroyd, from Burnley; the two Misses Denbigh, from the same place; a Miss Bolton, from Barrowford, and Miss Smith, her cousin, who married Mr. Willie Hallam, of Marsden Hall; Miss Armistead, of Wheatley Lane; the two Misses Grimshaw, of Crow Trees, Barrowford; the two Misses Phillips, of Greenfield; the Misses Ann and Fanny Watson, of Greenfield House; Miss Baldwin, of Spring House, who married Mr. T. Bolton, of Messrs. Bolton and Carr, solicitors; and the Misses Jane and Annie Earnshaw, of Craven Bank, Colne. There were many more, but these names come most readily to my memory. Some have, alas, passed away to the world of shadows. Still, there are some left who are doing God's work in this world, and these memories will remind them of the past happy days, ere the light of youth had faded.

> When the light of youth has faded,
> And gone are the happy years;
> When the path we tread is shaded,
> By old memories and their tears;
> It is then we find a pleasure,
> As our lives are flitting fast;
> In dreaming of the old days,
> When those old sweet days are past.

I was only a child of nine when we left Walk Mill and took a shop at the top of Windy Bank, next door to Mrs. Norton's pawnshop, and three doors from the Black Horse, in Church Street. It was in this house where my mother built up a famous confectionery and

funeral bread and biscuit bakery business. But
it was from Walk Mill—where, during the plug
drawing, my mother and grandmother, Jinny
Clitheroe, formerly Edmondson, daughter of Christopher Edmondson, who owned an old Colne
hostelry, the Masons' Arms, which stood in
Market Street, opposite the old coffee house—went to
meet the rioters on the Bridge, mentioned in Willie Bell's
"Memories of Colne." I cannot do better than quote
from this article, which lies before me now:—"How
many of Colne's inhabitants, I wonder, remember the
plug drawing? News came one Sunday that the rioters
were at Padiham. Then Mrs Ward—always a woman
of resource—gave orders that a fire should be lighted in
a large brick oven, and all Sunday night Mrs. Ward
and her mother worked, and, between them, baked a
pack of flour into cakes. When the rioters entered
Colne all the Ward's children were sent to a cottage,
called the Hagg, on the hill, out of harm's way. Then
all was bustle at Walk Mill. The cakes were cut up,
along with a large Cheshire cheese, and put into clothes
baskets, and covered with white clothes, and carried
to the bridge, where Mrs. Ward met the foremost rioter
—a tall, gaunt ruffian. 'What do you want?' she asked?
'We want a fair day's wage for a fair day's work,' he
shouted, brandishing a stick. 'Here, take this,' cried
the brave woman. 'Here is food, and a sum of money,
and I pray you do us no harm?' 'Nay, Missis,' he
shouted, 'tha's nooan a bad sooait, but we mon draw
plugs. Where's key?' Mr. Ward handed him the key,
with a request that it might be returned to him. The
plugs were drawn, and the key thrown into the middle
of the mill dam. But those troublous times are over
now. Many, very many, of the actors in this little
drama are sleeping the last sleep that knows no waking
beneath the shadows of the Old Church. There, too,
rests the brave woman who met the rioters on the
bridge." There, too, my brothers and sisters; I should
like to rest, when it shall please the Master to call His
servant home.

We will now walk once more, as in the old days, and
call on the shop-keepers from the toll bar at Guy Syke

to the toll bar at Dyson New Road, as it was called at that time, now Skipton-road. The first landlord of the Crown Hotel was a Mr. Hopkinson. Mrs. Hopkinson and her daughter were two very smart ladies, who opened a refreshment bar at the station. I used to take new milk and confectionery from our farm, the Old Colne Hall, every morning, and knew them well. There was also a refreshment house kept by a Mr. Leeming; it stood near the watering trough, where I used to take our cows to drink twice a day in winter time. He had a bill in the window, announcing that you could get ginger beer and a pot of tea and a bun; rather a strange mixture, if taken all at once, it seemed to me. A man, called Dean, kept the toll bar. The next shop was William Hardcastle's. He was the first to bring German barm into the town. There were no more houses until you reached the Parsonage. Opposite was Mrs. Walker's, then William Smith, joiner and builder. Then you came to the old building at Colne Hall. Here lived Johnny Boothman, and Jacky Briggs, an old pensioner, who had fought for the Motherland in the troublous days of Waterloo and had come back to lay his head to rest in the "Town upon the hill." Then we come to two old thatched cottages, where Old Peggy and her son lived, who wound bobbins for the dandy weavers at the bottom of Windy Bank. Next lived Joe and Betty Veevers, cap and straw bonnet trimmer, and coal carrier. Over on the opposite side lived Jude Baldwin, an old soldier, always most particular and clean in his dress. He wore white lambs' wool stockings and low shoes, polished like patent leather, and sold ale under the old Act. I do not remember any sign, only a few letters, "Licensed to sell ale." Next we came to a large garden by the road side; after that a stone yard. Then Thomas Ward's (my father's and mother's home) at the corner of Spring Lane. It stands there still, but there were no other houses near it; only a stone and sand yard. On the opposite side stood the house and shop of John Cork, grocer and reed maker; on the other side, Dean's cloth warehouse. Wm. Wilkinson and Son, wholesale grocers; then came Dr. Buck's house, and Miss Ibbotson, ladies' dressmaker (long since dead and gone, I am told); Miss Cockcroft's confectioner's shop; then Kellett, the tailor, who used to take his sons out for a walk every morning before eight o'clock; so punctual was he that my mother used to say to us "It's 8 o'clock; there's Mr. Kellett and his boys gone up the road." After Kellett's was Mrs. Baldwin's shop, just opposite the chapel. Then came Hartley Hurst's, clogger and shoe maker; then the cottage of Harry Horsfall, German barm dealer, and father of the present Lady Pickles Hartley; and next door to Horsfall's lived Betty Wilkinson, who kept a little toffee shop. Then came Vipond's, shoemaker, and across the way Bottomley's, painters and decorators; then the post office. John Asquith was postmaster in those days; a very smart man, I used to think, when he walked out with his family on a Sunday afternoon. Next came Starkey, grocer and flour dealer; and Butler and Sons, high-class tailors, and opposite was the Golden Ball, an old-fashioned beerhouse, where the older generation of Colne damped their clay, when dry. Next to Butler's was Tom Young's, the butcher. Next, the King's Head, kept by John Hilary, and opposite stood the Derby Arms, long since removed elsewhere. After that was Baldwin's, the stationer's. Next came the church, that dear old church where my mother and father sleep while still ebbs and flows the busy life of the old place; where still, Sunday after Sunday, the sons and daughters of old Colne kneel to our Father in Heaven Who is the Father of us all, where, Sunday after Sunday, the old bells ring out over the surrounding hills: "Come all to church, good people; good people, come and pray."

CHAPTER II.

"Come all to church, good people; good people, come and pray." And they went to church, in those days, rich and poor alike, side by side; the rich always with a kindly smile of welcome for his poorer brethren, for Dives did not despise Lazarus when we all sat under the

Ex-Ald. S. Catlow, J.P.
Colne's First Mayor.

Sir W. P. Hartley,
Colne's First Knight.

Rev. John Henderson,
Colne's First Rector.

Dr. Ayre,
Colne's First Factory Certifying Surgeon.

Alkincoats Hall, home to the Parker family who owned considerable land and property in Colne; the Parkers Arms was their inn. Their estate covered 800–900 acres, including several farms: Hobstones, Edge End, Great House and Colne Edge. Colne Council bought the hall and grounds in 1921 and it was demolished in 1957. It was here that Elizabeth Shackleton, nee Parker, wrote much of her diary in the eighteenth century.

Heirs House was originally the home of Abraham Hargreaves, one of the earliest cotton men. Later this house was enlarged into a fine mansion by Thomas Thornber England, a member of an influential local family who owned Spring Gardens Mill which burnt to the ground in 1875, one of the most spectacular mill fires in Colne.

great pulpit and listened to the voice of our loved minister, who was in very truth to us the ambassador of God. Sweet, old-world spot, resting place of those that made life dear when life was young; here and there a tombstone marks the last resting place of some long dead and almost forgotten friend, who at one time lived, moved and had his being in their midst, whose laughter rang through the streets, who knew thee and thine through boyhood, youth, manhood, and age, but now lies at rest under the shadow of the Old Church, "Waiting for God to call." Over him and the friends of his youth the bells ring out merrily, or may-be one rings out to tell the sleepers another life has departed. Do they hear it, I wonder! Ah, me; well, forgive an old woman's musings.

It was under the shadow of the Old Church and on the path of that daisy-starred "God's Acre" that we children used to stand on a Sunday morning, dressed in our "best bibs and tuckers," and watch all the grand folks come to church. How proud we were when some great lady would smile on us when passing! Old Mr. Parker, J.P., and his son, Captain Parker, came regularly from Alkincoates; also the family, in their carriage, from Browsholme, and children and any visitors that might be staying with them at the time. How they rustled by, in their beautiful silks and lace shawls! The hair was worn in long ringlets over the ears, and fell in ripples on the shoulders. There was one tall lady of some 50 summers (who shall be nameless) who simpered and smiled and shook her finger and curls at you in a playful kittenish manner, just like the youngest Miss Pecksniff. I remember I used to go home and make my mother smile when I mimicked her. And my poor mother, worried with the cares of a business, would laugh and say, "When our Jane comes in she makes me feel young again."

Then came Mr. and Mrs. England, from Heirs House, with Miss England and her brothers, Tom and Nicholas. Miss England and her brother had been abroad, had visited Jerusalem and seen the Temple. In my childish dreams I visited that Temple many times, and it seemed strange to me that someone I knew had seen the very place where Our Lord had lived and preached. For in those days Jerusalem seemed so very far away; almost out of the world, in fact; but now, in these days of Cook's tours, it seems almost at our city gates, and, as we near the end of our lives, Jesus Himself comes nearer, too.

Then there came Mr. and Mrs. Carr, of Langroyd, and their children; Dr. Ayre and family; Mr. George Carr and sister, Miss Fidelea; the Misses Bolton, Mr. Holmes (solicitor), and his lady, and Mr. Wood, J.P., and his daughter, from the Craggs. I have heard a touching story of the devotion of a faithful old servant of this family. They were, I believe, very wealthy at one time, kept hunters and rode to hounds; but reverses came to them, as it has done to many of the "stately homes of England." When things were at the worst this faithful old domestic came to her master and said, "Don't you bother, sir; they shan't have everything. I'll see to that." So, when affairs were smoothed over and settled, she took her master into the yard (or fold, as it was called) and, tipping over the swill tub, said "There, sir, what do you think of that?" And there lay all the valuable family plate; some of it heirlooms, bright and glittering in the sunshine, and as good as new; an act of devotion it would be hard to beat. But servants were servants in those days, who studied their employers' interests as their own.

Many of the best tradesmen atended the Old Church, but we will take them one by one, as we wander through the street. Our pew was in the chancel, near the altar rails. I'm afraid that, child-like, my mind wandered away very often from what the minister was saying. I just loved to watch the ladies rustling by in their silks and graceful hanging shawls.

The Parkers' (of Alkincoates) pew was next to ours, and Mr. Holmes (of Hardacre and Holmes) had a large square pew lined with scarlet cloth and edged with brass nails. Away from us sat the two Misses Bolton and their mother, a sweet-faced lady, and Mr. Waddington

Hartley and two children (boy and girl) had a large pew on the opposite side.

In a pew not far from us one summer, sat a lady and a boy; visitors, I think. The boy used to smile at me, and I, girl like, smiled back. You see the little god Cupid can even be found in Colne Church. I wonder if he attends the services still. I think he must, or why those smiles and merry greetings outside the gates at night, when service is over? Ah, me! It was all so sweet and young, and now so far away.

Our minister was the Rev. John Henderson. He had two sons, James and Leonard. James married a lady rather well endowed with this world's goods, and brought her to Colne. For a time all seemed fair and prosperous, but the childish lips that had lisped the prayer, "Our Father," and had been taught to worship at the altar of the living God by a father who was himself a disciple of Christ, became in manhood a worshipper at the shrine of Bacchus, and the young life that had opened in all the peace and serenity of a minister's household ended in the gloom and squalor of a lodging-house in Windy Bank. Leonard married his father's maid-servant, who was a daughter of old Dick Lancaster, the sexton, who tolled the bell only at the deaths. I remember my mother saying to me when my father died, "Jane, run and tell old Dick Lancaster to ring the bell"; and presently, over the houses of old Colne, the bell tolled out mournfully, to tell the people another life had departed—a quaint, old-world custom, and one of those that might have been left us. Talking of bells, in my young days the curfew rang at 6 o'clock in the morning and 8 o'clock in the evening. The shop-keepers waited to hear the bell before putting up their shutters.

The first curate that I remember was a Mr. Perrin, a genial Irishman, always ready with a joke or a laugh. Mr. Perrin was a great favourite with the young ladies of Colne, who knitted him lambs' wool socks, and made him woolwork slippers. He was great at bazaars and "tea-fights." Mr. Perrin liked tea, but—(hush)—he liked something in it. Now, while Mr. Perrin took tea all went well, because "what the eye don't see the heart don't grieve." But when Mr. Perrin began to take the (something) without the tea, well, as the saying is, "All the fat was in the fire," and he had to go. Poor fellow. Everyone was sorry for him. The next curate was a Mr. Owen, who must have been all that could be desired. He stayed many years.

The first clerk of the church I remember was a very old man, who gave the responses at quite inopportune moments. I remember he cried out "Amen" at the end of a fit of sneezing once, and, of course, everyone laughed. The next one was, I think, called Horsfield.

The weddings at the Old Church were notable events. When Miss Parker, of Alkincoates, was married, the bridegroom threw handfuls of money away, and it was great fun watching the people scramble for it. Another great event was Mr. William Bracewell's wedding to Miss Mary Whittaker. How beautiful she looked in her cream satin and orange blossoms! "Just like a wax doll," someone said. Now, to be compared to a wax doll may not be very complimentary; but still, wax dolls have lovely complexions; so had Miss Whittaker. It was like cream and roses.

The funniest wedding I ever saw at the Old Church was that of (we'll call them, Jock and Jenny). They had got to where the clergyman says "Put on the ring." Jock was nervous, and in his agitation could not remember where he had put it. Pocket after pocket was searched. The friends of the bride and bridegroom crowded round. "Where did ta' put it?" said the bride, almost in tears. "Here, in this pocket," said Jock, holding up the side of his coat. He felt again, and called out gleefully "It's here." "Put on the ring," said the clergyman again. The bride held up her by-no-means dainty finger. The ring refused to go over the knuckle, but Jock had had enough and did not intend to stop at trifles. He just shoved the bride's finger into his mouth, licked it, and it was done. Even our good clergyman smiled. During the wedding break-fast someone, of a religious turn of mind, said that

The Crown Hotel, Albert Road, c1906. Albert Road was previously known as Manchester Road and prior to that as Westgate. The Crown Hotel on the left of the picture was built to cater for the custom of the railway. The first landlord was a Mr. Hopkinson, whose wife and daughter – two very smart ladies – opened a refreshment bar at the station. The tall building on the left was the police station and courthouse built in the 1870s, and across the road was the Post Office.

Albert Road. On the right of the picture is the Town Hall, built in 1894; opposite is the Wesleyan Chapel whose foundation stone was laid on 1ˢᵗ April 1824 on a bitterly cold day with snow on the ground. The present St. John's Church on the same site was opened on the 11ᵗʰ May 1968.

Market Days in Colne must have seen a great deal of waiting about – Fridays was livestock day, and cattle would be tethered to any convenient post and the farmers would mill around striking bargains; for the ladies the cattle wouldn't have been the only obstacles on the roads. On market days the inns and alehouse had extended opening hours and the day's activities were often associated with drunken revelry.

Albert Road and the top of Spring Lane – a good day's work.

"Marriages were made in heaven." "Oh, are they?" said the bridegroom. "If aw'm to be wed ageean like that, aw'm noan bahn."

But the merriest and most picturesque weddings were those from Barrowford. How often have I stood on the road between the toll bar and the Parsonage and watched them go by. First came a fiddler, decorated with many-coloured ribbons, and playing a merry tune. After him came the bridal party — as often as not a bright, rosy-faced country lad and lass. If the groom had had a taste of "John Barleycorn" that morning he would jig it along the road with the best of them, and the maid would daintily raise her flowered muslin and trip it by his side. There was the usual good-humoured banter, and the "God bless you" when it was over, and the fiddler struck up his merry tune again as they crossed the road and entered the White Horse Inn, after one of the Grammar School boys had said the homily, and received a piece of silver from the bridegroom and a smile from the blushing bride; while the old bells rang out a parting peal.

CHAPTER III.

I am thinking, I am thinking,
And my eyes are dim with tears,
Of the days that knew not sadness,
In the dim and distant years.
In the firelight's dying embers,
Flit the scenes from days of yore,
Age, with joy, its youth remembers,
Dear dead days that are no more.

The White Horse Inn stood exactly opposite the church gates. It was an old-fashioned whitewashed house, with narrow Gothic windows, and a passage in the centre which ran from front to back, wide enough for a horse and cart to pass through. How often I have stood as a girl and gazed through that passage across the sunlit fields and the hills beyond,

And have seen the shadows falling,
In the evening of the day;
And have heard the old world calling,
"Come away, child, come away."

My father remembered seeing the churchwardens go into this house with their long poles during church hours, and bring the customers out to attend service. I myself remember Old Lancaster, the sexton, coming out with a stick, pounce upon a crowd of rebellious boys, and lug a couple of them into church, while the others danced round like wild Indians, and shouted "Let 'em go, you old beggar, let 'em go." And, as often as not, they attempted a rescue. What would our latter day parents say at such usage of their offspring, when even a teacher cannot chastise an unruly scholar without fear of police court proceedings? The old White Horse Inn stood so near the channel, or gutter, as we called it, that people had to wait until a cart had passed before they could pass themselves.

A sad fatality happened here during my girlhood. One afternoon a little child was standing near the wall of the house as a cart was passing. The carter being on the side of the cart nearest the church did not notice the child's danger. There was a shout from some men, and a horrified scream from some women standing near. The cart passed on, and the poor little child sank to the ground, dead, with its head crushed against the wall of the house. The tragedy caused a sensation at the time. On the day of the funeral the little martyr's coffin was covered with flowers.

Next door to the White Horse lived Miss Stevenson, a dressmaker, and her brother, a tailor. Miss Stevenson, when in Burnley one day, saw in a Manchester Road shop window a card, which read:— "Miss Hyde, Modes." A few days afterwards a similar card appeared in Miss Stevenson's window. A well-known solicitor saw it, and smiled. Miss Stevenson came out at this moment. "Good morning, Miss Stevenson," said he. "Good morning, Mr. So-and-so," said Miss Stevenson. "You have a new card in your window," said he.

"Yes," replied the lady. "Modes," he said, reflectively. "What does it mean?" "It means dressmaker," answered Miss Stevenson. "Indeed," said the gentleman, smiling, "then if I were you I'd write it in plain English. We don't all understand French." "Then I pity your ignorance," snapped Miss Stevenson, as she bounced in and shut the door. A day or two afterwards "Modes" vanished, and the old familiar card, "Miss Stevenson, dressmaker," appeared again.

In the next house lived Jimmy Wilkinson and his two daughters. The father and one daughter were the shortest people in Colne, just like dwarfs. They made a very fair living, however, selling pots and salt—a kind of marine store. After this was the shop of Robert Smith, joiner and cabinet maker. He always had a good stock of solid, substantial furniture in. There was a large family of the Smith's. The boys Tom and William learnt their father's trade, and were true friends of my brothers Jonathan and William. John and Harry were apprenticed to Mr. Richmond, ironmonger in the town, and after marriage settled in Leeds. The next house was the Fleece Inn, kept by Robert Jackson, a wood sawyer by trade. Then came the Parker's Arms.

It was on the opposite side, near the higher church gates, where the old stocks which were brought from the police station yard used to be placed. I have seen both men and women in them at the same time. The punishment of the stocks was usually inflicted on market days. The culprits sat with their faces towards the church-yard, quite near the gates, while the police walked up and down continually, to keep order. One day I saw a huge crowd swaying and pushing, and, girl-like, I ran up to see what was the matter. A man and woman were in the stocks. The woman I recognised as one who had been drunk outside the King's Arms the night before, and had amused the crowd by dancing a hornpipe. The man looked downcast and ashamed. The woman—a red-faced, jolly looking wench—saw a farmer in the crowd smoking a clay pipe and asked him for a draw. The farmer good naturedly stopped and put the pipe into the woman's mouth. She puffed away contentedly for a few moments while the crowd laughed and joked. Then, turning to her companion in misfortune, she put the pipe into his mouth, saying, "Have a draw, owd lad." It was a comical scene; it is sixty years since I saw it, yet it remains as keen in my memory as though it happened but yesterday.

There was a passage through the stoops at the front of the Grammar School. The school, you must remember, was in full swing then, under the headmastership of Mr. Harrison, a worthy man and a great scholar. How many old Colne boys to-day have kindly memories of their old teacher, whose voice is now as still and silent as the old school itself, once the scene of so much youth, gaiety and life? My brothers were, all four of them, educated there, William and Jonathan under Mr. Harrison, Edmondson and John under a former master, whose name I have forgotten. Bazaars, magic lanterns and even lotteries used to be held in the top room above the school, reached by the steps leading up from outside. I believe lotteries are now considered illegal, but they helped many a poor man and woman to keep a home together during the bad times in the old days. I remember my brother William coming home with a couple of pictures he had won at one of them. The tickets were 6d. each, and the pictures were probably worth about 5s. each. The subjects were "Christ blessing bread," and "A scene from the battle of Waterloo," a soldier loading a cannon, with the dead and dying around. He told us there had been 60 tickets sold; a nice little sum this for a man out of work who had hit upon this mode of "raising the wind."

Now, we will walk up as far as the Craven Bank, kept by Mr. Joseph Earnshaw and one clerk. How different the scene to-day! The new clock over the arch used to be lighted up by Fred Hirst, the shoemaker. "Owd Ned," he was called, and father of Thomas Hirst, the chemist. Then there was Mr Charnley's shop, chemist and druggist. He was a bachelor, and lived with his mother and one servant maid. I can see him

The Parsonage, Albert Road. One of the earliest residents was Rev. John Henderson. He was very well liked by both church and chapel and when the fiftieth anniversary of his incumbency was celebrated in 1869, everyone turned out to do him honour. In his spare time his hobby was making and flying kites. Locally the house was never known as the Rectory.

The Cloth Hall opened for business on Christmas Day, 1775. The land it was built on was provided by Banastre Walton of Marsden; it was here local handloom weavers sold their woven cloth pieces. In later years it served as a market, a store house, a dance hall, a meeting room and a barracks. Troops were stationed here from 1840 and their presence helped bring stability to Colne, their red uniforms bringing a splash of colour to the town.

Stocks – In 1822 the old stone stocks that had stood at the top of Colne were removed as they were becoming a hazard to coaches, along with the market cross and the town well. The new stocks that replaced them were constructed with iron wheels, reputedly by Hartley Smith. The stocks were kept in the police station yard and trundled out whenever needed. They were taken as far as Brierfield for the punishment of offenders who were jeered and spat at by self righteous residents of the town. The stocks ceased to be used in the late 1850s or early 1860s. Pictured on the right is PC Richard Shaw and three locals posing as malefactors, the stocks can now be viewed in Colne Heritage Centre at Colne Library.

now in my mind's eye, in his white linen apron, spotlessly clean. His shop was like Rimmell's in the Strand. You knew you were nearing Charnley's by the perfume in the street. I heard after his death that he had left his housekeeper a pound a week for life. I hope it is true, but it is not often faithful service is rewarded in this world.

Then we pass a leather shop; name over the window, Nuttall. (Remember we are having a stroll between 50 and 60 years ago, so don't expect to see a motor dash round the corner. A motor; why, people had scarcely got used to trains). Now we come to where Mrs. Goddard and her three daughters, milliners, lived. What smart girls they were. Alice was a Sunday school teacher, but one Sunday no teacher arrived, and, like the maid in the old ballad, "The misletoe bough,"

> They sought her that night,
> And they sought her next day,
> And they sought her for weeks,
> Till a year passed away.

But long before a week had passed away, news came. Miss Goddard had eloped, with a blind music teacher. Contrary to the gossips, it turned out a happy marriage, for she called with her husband, Mr. Bracewell, to see my sister some years ago. They were then living near London with a wealthy old aunt, who was childless, and drove out in a pony phaeton every day. So it all turned out for the best.

Then there was Hudson's (the draper's) shop on the opposite side, and a smart-looking wholesale and retail tea and coffee shop, not grocery, kept by Emery Howarth, son of Caleb Howarth, the Quaker, who lived at Nelson and came to Colne every day. He wore black stockings and breeches, and looked saintly. It seemed to me that old Caleb had something to do with the law. I may be wrong, but I often saw him hurrying up Albert Road on market days, carrying a lawyer's brief bag. His daughter-in-law, wife of Emery, was a tall lady-like person, with a condescending manner, and a sweet smile.

B

Next door was T. Holt's smallware shop, he being
by trade a blacksmith. The daughter, Elizabeth Holt,
was a great friend of mine. We were in the same class
at the Sunday school taught by Miss Minnie Bolton.
Next was Stephen Wooley's grocery business. His son
Stephen went to Burnley and worked at Arnold's wool
warehouse in the town, and, like Whittington of old,
married his master's daughter, and had a family. One
of the daughters is now Mrs. Pate, widow of Mr. Pate,
hairdresser, of Howe Street, Burnley. I do not know
what became of Mary Jane Wooley, daughter of old
Stephen. She was an accomplished girl, could play the
piano, and sang nicely — a rare accomplishment at that
time. I remember that piano well. It was like a table,
and on a brass tablet in front it said "Maker to His
Majesty, and the young princesses."

CHAPTER IV.

Across old Colne Hall fields,
We roamed with dallying feet;
Or merrily scaled the wall below,
To watch the mill dam's rushing flow.
Whate'er the future holds, I know
Those olden days were sweet.
Around me Colne lies fair,
The sunset flecked with gold.
I hear the sound of children's feet,
I hear the sound of laughter sweet.
Oh, near that church I used to meet
My love in the days of old.
And there, just as of old,
The mills are working still;
On many a bright and summer day,
With friends now long since passed away,
My heart, in memory, loves to stray,
O'er "Colne upon the Hill."

Well, gentle reader, we will now walk up as far as
Colne Lane. But, first of all, I must tell you I have had

a visit from an old friend of my girlhood's days. She is now Mrs. Duerden, formerly Miss Asquith, daughter of the late postmaster of Colne. She came in, and we had a talk about old times and old friends long since dead and gone. She had been reading these "Memories." "Do you like them?" I asked? "Like them," she said; "we do, and the best of it is, it's all true." Well, that pleased me, for I want to write nothing but what is true, and nothing but what has happened to my own personal knowledge. I asked about Elizabeth Asquith. Dear Elizabeth; what friends we were in the old days! She married a smart, good looking young fellow, called George Bulcock. I remember calling for her one evening when we were girls, and finding her in the midst of Spring cleaning. I said "Do you expect George to-night, Elizabeth?" "Of course," she replied, "catch him miss; he'll come." "Well," said I, "are you going to see him like that?" "Of course," was the answer, with a toss of the head. "If he won't have me rough, he'll not get me smooth." But they did get married, and if ever there was a love match theirs was one. Elizabeth, like the writer of these "Memories," is a widow, and I love to think that when the one clear call comes for us those whom in our youth we loved, and who have only gone a little while before, will be waiting to welcome the wanderers home.

Well, the next place we come to is Hartley Earnshaw's (father of Joseph Earnshaw, of Craven Bank), printer and stationer. It was a very old-fashioned shop, with two windows, and the door in the centre. On the tops of the counters which ran up either side of the shop were cases of visiting and wedding cards, Bibles and Prayer Books. There was an air of superiority about the place 60 years ago which included the young lady who served behind the counter. She was a Miss Ellison, who married a Mr. Hartley, from Pendle Forest. A Miss Cockcroft was her successor. She remained many years.

Next was a very old house, a relic of old Colne. A low stone wall ran down the front and side, on which the youngsters of "Colunio" climbed to watch a wild beast or circus procession go past whenever they visited the town. The yard was covered with rough paving stones, and you went up a stone step into the shop. This was old Jacky Hardacre's fruit and treacle toffee shop. Oh, that treacle toffee ; beloved of the youngsters of Colne! How many young feet, now grown weary with the pilgrimage of life, have pattered over those paving stones, and through that low doorway, there to find a haven of bliss in the perfume of treacle toffee, as often as not bubbling and sizzling on the fire? Well, old Jacky has gone, and his house has vanished, to give place to what are termed improvements. Ah, well; but give me the old days, with their quiet home life and simple pleasures, when our Good Queen Victoria was young, and having her children, and when every fresh birth was an excuse for the lighting of bonfires, the ringing of bells, and a burst of honest English gladness that another bonnie bairn had come to gladden the heart of the best queen, the best mother, and the best woman in the world. And who is there amongst us to-day that does not give the same love to the son we gave to the mother? Ah; we do that; so we'll shake hands on it.

Well, the next we come to was Mr. Wilson's, bread baker; then Smith, saddler and harness maker; then, just at the top of Colne Lane, and over the saddler's shop, lived Joe Rushton, the clogger. He reached his house by a sort of "Jacob's ladder" arrangement, up a flight of stone steps, and through a door. I have taken my clogs there to be clogged, but never explored the interior of the Rushton abode.

Now we'll start at the Craven Bank again, and walk up on the opposite side. The first past the bank was Mrs. Holroyd's millinery establishment. She had three daughters (stylish girls they were, too) and one son. One of the daughters married Mr. Darnborough, and had one son. I do not remember whom the others married. Then we came to Betty Booth's bread shop. She was a bread baker in a large way, and supplied many of the soldiers with bread when Colne was a garrison town and the barracks were in the Cloth Hall. Subscription balls and parties were also held in this old building. My brother Jonathan told me rather a funny story about one of these balls, which, I think, will bear repeating. One night one of the red-coated revellers on his way home met a well-known local preacher. I fear the soldier's language (according to Jonathan) was rather lurid, so the preacher went up to him and said: "My friend, have you found salvation?" "No," hiccoughed the lad in red, "but I can tell thee where tha can find Sall Johnson." She was one of those ladies whom Swinburne meant when he wrote,

> Cold eyelids, that hide like a jewel,
> Hard eyes, that grow soft for an hour.

But to return to Betty Booth. Her bakehouse was in the Church Ginnell. She had a finely built young fellow helping her as baker, named Dick Stansfield. He afterwards married, and had a bakery business in St. James' Street, Burnley. I saw him when quite an old man carrying a tray of steaming hot bread through Burnley streets, just as he used to do in his youth 40 years before, when he carried Betty Booth's bread from the Church Ginnell to her shop. She was a clever, bustling, business woman, with a merry word for the soldier laddies when they came with their large hampers for bread in the mornings, calling on their way at Jacky Hardacre's for vegetables, and returning to the Barracks heavily laden. Morning, noon, and night Betty used to be at her post, with a smile here and a kind word there, and a "buttie" for the bairns. One day one of the "unco guid" asked her why she worked so hard to amass money, when it was "the root of all evil." "Oh," she said, "it's the root of all evil, is it? All right, owd lad, awm bahn to have a little bit more of that root." Ah, well, I think we could all do with a bit more of that root. What do you say?

The next place was Hartley Gossling's, barber and hairdresser. He was a little dark man, with a wife to match. They had two children, George and Harriet, who carried the shop on when their parents died. Harriet used to lather the customers for her father. I remember we made up a bit of rhyme about it. It ran:

Harriet, tha shall not go an' play,
To that aw'll noan agree;
For if tha will not lather customers,
Why then, aw'll lether thee.

The next was Dr. Buck's house. He had two sons, Henry and Edward, both doctors, and two daughters as well. He was such a kind, sympathetic man, and attended my own mother in all her trouble. The next was Oates Patterson's butcher's shop. He was a little, stout, red-faced, funny man. He lived just at the corner of Windy Bank, but after Patterson's was Heaton's, chemist and druggist, uncle of Mr. Heaton, chemist, of Burnley. Then came the Black Horse beerhouse, long since vanished; then John Ayre's, the joiner; and then my own home, Mrs. Ward's, grocer and confectioner, and Miss Mary Ward, milliner and straw bonnet maker. My sister Mary lived for some years with Mrs. Helm, wife of Elijah Helm, and married Benjamin Rawson. She was afterwards for some years landlady of the Griffin Hotel, Burnley, and died there respected and loved by all who came in contact with her. Mrs. Norton's pawnshop, as the Colne people called it, was close to our shop. I have seen quite well-to-do people call to see their "uncle"; perhaps I ought to say "aunt" in this case. Aye; and those whom one would think could never be in want of a shilling have slipped in at that side door. God help them, is all I can say. They'd better do that than ask relatives, and God bless the banker of the poor.

The next shop, at the corner of Colne Lane, was Matthew Cragg's, tea dealer. While he travelled for orders his cousin, Miss Margaret Cragg, attended to the shop. They both lived with Mrs. Parkinson, who was their aunt, and had a little shop down Windy Bank, and she was the mother of the great Parkinson, pill and baking-powder maunfacturer, of Curzon Street, Burnley, and one of Colne's noblest captains of industry. My sister Mary and Miss Cragg were bosom friends, and in their spare time often chatted in our shop. Then I was sent over to look after Miss Cragg's shop, because "little pigs have big ears," you know. Well, one night, Mary Ann Norton and I were sent over as usual. The shop was decorated for Christmas with holly and mistletoe. The red berries looked tempting. I sampled a few. Time passed. I began to have a sort of "all-overish" feeling. Mary Ann Norton looked scared, and said they were poison. I began to cry, and ran over home, and told them what I had done. My sister screamed. Miss Cragg flopped down on to a chair, and gasped, "How many have you eaten?" "Eight or nine," I answered. "Oh, Lord," said my sister, "she's done for." Then my mother, hearing the commotion, came in. "Whatever's to do?" she asked. They told her. "Here," she said, "take this pot and run to Heaton's and tell him. He'll gi' thi something." I showed him the berries. He opened one, and said, "Be quick and run home, drink this, and have some hot tea." Presently the berries made their appearance a second time on earth; had it been otherwise I should have made my exit from it. How I do rattle on, to be sure. Well, you shouldn't have set me on, for, when once an old Colner starts talking about the dear old town, she never knows when to stop.

CHAPTER V.

Ah me, how my old memories bite to-night as I write. My sister's friend, Miss Cragg, married Mr. Bolton, of Nelson, and became the mother of the Bolton Brothers, wholesale grocers, Elizabeth Street, Burnley. After Matthew Cragg's tea-shop, we come to a gentlewoman's hatter's shop, name of Barker. Mrs. Barker was the daughter of Barnard Crook, who had a cloth and fustian business on the opposite side. But we will have a chat about him as we stroll up the left side of the street. Mr. Darnborough lived in the next house, and now we come to the "Hole in the Wall," kept, when I was a girl, by Betty Anderton. Miss Betty Anderton, don't forget. She believed in single blessedness. So do I—

now. Betty had many chances, but she told them all
she'd consider about it, and write, and immediately they
got a letter they were to come at once, as she didn't like
to be kept waiting when she was in that way. But Betty
was sensible, and died as she had lived, dear, good-
hearted, plain Betty Anderton. Would there were
more to-day like her. She kept two maids and a man,
Amos Harker. Who did not know Amos? Amos, with
his sleeves rolled up, ready for work, either in the house
or in the yard. The Royal Mail put up at the "Hole
in the Wall," after leaving the mail bags at the Post
Office, at 8 o'clock in the morning until 8 o'clock at
night. What stirring times those were! There stand
the grand old coach and a couple of horses, fresh as
daisies after their rest. The guard is there with his
horn, ready to give a "Root, toot, toot." The coachman,
a red-faced jolly chap, raises his whip. "Let 'em go,
Amos," he cries. The stable helpers fly back, drawing
the cloths off the horses' glossy flanks, and away they
go down Albert-road, the guard blowing his horn like
mad, and the errand boys rushing out to see the mail
go by. The housemaids smile from the upper windows,
and the tradesmen stand in groups and wonder how long
it will take them to reach Burnley. Well, dear readers,
how do you like the picture? Isn't it far better than
what we have now? Stuffy railway stations, and a
uniformed guard to look after our mails? Isn't the
picture of the old Mail Coach outside the "Hole in the
Wall" far healthier and better, and more like the dear
old England of our fathers than the present system?
Of course it is, and that's my opinion, and yours as well,
I know, and we don't intend to alter it, do we?

Well; come along. The next was Whittaker and
Dixon's, ironmongers and tin-plate workers. The Miss
Mary Whittaker whom I saw married at the Old Church
was the daughter of the head of this firm. Now we
come to the Swan Hotel, or, as it was familiarly called,
"Snowden's." I remember the old house well. I mean
the one that stood on the site of the present building.
Old houses are always cosy and home-like. So was this,
with its large kitchen and its long settle that stood by

Mr. F. Richmond,
Chairman of the old Colne Education Committee.

Ex-Ald. William Sagar, J.P.,
Colne's First County Councillor.

Mr. Wm. Hewitt.

Mr. S. Greenwood,
One of Colne's First Guardians.

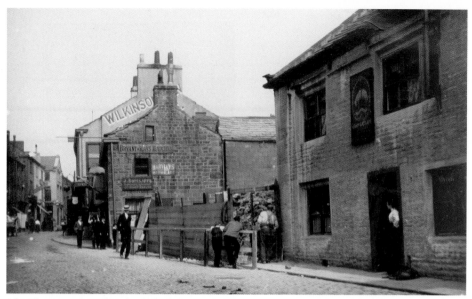

The Fleece Inn on Church Street was an inn traditionally associated with the woollen weavers and the Cloth Hall. On the right of the picture can be seen Wilkinson's chemist and Veevers' confectioners shops.

Church Street was a lot wider until the building of the new Ivegate by Nicholas England in 1841, with the town clock which lasted until 1875. Ivegate, its name meaning 'road to the water', used to be the ancient lane which led to the church well near the Parish Church.

the side of the fire. I remember one winter's night my brother and I were sent with a note to Mr. Snowden. One of the maids was bathing the children by the kitchen fire. The new front had just been built into the house, and planks were laid down for pedestrians to walk on; but before the house was finished two of Mrs. Snowden's bonnie bairns were called away to Our Father in Heaven, and only one boy, Joseph (who years afterwards became landlord of the Swan), was left. I knew his sisters, Sarah Ann and Jane Snowden. Well, Charlie Butler, the son of Butler, the high-class tailor in Church Street, taught dancing in those days, and gave the Snowden girls two private lessons a week. Mrs. Snowden kindly gave us permission to learn as well, if we provided lights. So, behold us sallying forth, like the virgins of Biblical history, not with our lights burning, but with two enormous wax candles ready to light. And the dances. Well, we did not glide, bend, and twirl like Maude Allen, nor do a serpentine dance like Loie Treller, nor a skirt dance like graceful Kate Vaughan. Oh, no. Why, the older generation of Colne would have thought us clean daft. We just had a rattling good country dance, which flushed the cheeks and stirred the blood, and made us all feel the better for it afterwards. Well, when the house was finished, Mrs. Snowden determined to give a sort of children's party and dance, and the great question at home was, "What has our Jane to wear?" Mother wanted to buy me a new dress, but Edmondson said "No, we are not going to that expense." Then my grandmother said, "She is called after me, and she shall have my wedding dress." So it was brought out of a chest—a beautiful green silk, all smelling of lavender—and duly inspected. Then Margaret Edmondson was called in. She was a dressmaker, and daughter of David Edmondson, who fought at Waterloo. Margaret Edmondson married twice. Her first husband was called Snowden, and kept the toll bar at Wycollar. Her second husband's name was Spencer. She buried them both, and in talking of them she used to say, with a rougish look in her eyes, "Ah, well, they're better off. I know I am. They both left me a bit of money." Well,

Margaret declared the dress splendid. So it was cut up, and little Jane Ward went to Snowden's ball in her grandmother's wedding dress.

Margaret Edmondson went with her father, David (then an old man), to London, to see the Great Exhibition, in 1851, with one or two more friends from Colne. They found themselves in the guard room at Windsor Castle one afternoon. A few soldiers stood around. The old man looked, but looked in vain for a familiar face. For it was in this very room, where, 36 years before, he and his merry companions, in all the splendour of their hot and restless youth, had received, with a shout of gladness, the news that their regiment had been ordered to the seat of war, to fight for the dear old homeland. He looked at one or two grizzled veterans, and very nearly spoke to them. Then he thought "They're all gone, all gone, and no one to remember me." He stood on the very spot where he had stood 36 years before, when the news came. Oh, where was that bright-faced lad in the red coat who had stood by his side that morning? They were inseparable then. Oh, gone, dead and gone, and laid in a soldier's grave. He conjured up the scene till he could almost hear the shouts of his companions, and the crashing of the shells on the field of Waterloo, for memory was crowding his brain. And beneath his worn soldier's tunic his brave old heart was throbbing with a sense of loss, of loneliness, and a dim yearning for "the touch of a vanish'd hand, and the sound of a voice that was still." He looked helplessly round. Then, turning to his daughter, he leaned his head on his arm and wept —

> "Wept for his lost companions,
> Fond-hearted, true and brave,
> Who had saluted the last outpost
> On the frontier of the grave."

As I said before, David sleeps in Colne Churchyard.

Snowden's Yard, or the Croft, is, as everyone knows, where the Fair was held, but the Fairs of 60 years ago and those of the present day are two totally different affairs. There were, of course, swings, roundabouts,

penny shows, and peep-shows, where it was, according
to the dress of the ladies, eternal summer. But the
roundabouts were not worked by steam, but were set
going by men running at the side of the cars, and
horses, and shoving them round. One or two, more
advanced, were worked by a man turning a handle in
the centre, similar to a grindstone. And the lights
were the old-fashioned flaring oil lamps. There were,
of course, the usual stalls of toys, gingerbread, and
snaps; the old barrel organs grinding out the popular
tunes of the day; the penny theatre, where you could see
"Maria Martin," or "The murder in the Red Barn,"
"Sweeney Todd," "The Demon Barber of Fleet Street,"
and one or two other equally blood-curdling dramas.
There were fat women and two-headed snakes, and pigs
who told your fortunes by alphabetical cards. There
were waxwork shows, and you could have your likeness
taken on black paper stuck on a white card, and in a
sort of frame, all for 3d. The Fair was not confined
to Snowden Yard, for stalls were spread out all down
Church Street, and pot auctions were held at the top
of Colne Lane. The Fair week was a time of re-union
of sundered families, and long absent friends, for, come
what might, all tried to get home during that time.
There were not then the rush and worry of business there
are to-day. At any rate, people seemed to look forward
to their holidays with a greater zest, and to have more
time for enjoyment of the old pastime.

At the left-hand corner, as you entered Snowden
Yard, 60 years ago, stood an old-fashioned house, called
Sugden's Coffee House. The house, a relic of olden
times, had two windows facing up the street, and a side
door facing the Masons' Arms, an old-fashioned public-
house — now, like so many objects of interest of our dear
old town, a thing of the past. There were two rooms
on the ground floor, where basins of coffee were served
on market days. I have seen the place crowded with
farmers and market women on Wednesdays and Saturdays. There was a large whitewashed brick oven by
the side of a huge fire, where a kettle, hung by a chain
from the chimney, was in a state of perpetual boil.

Mrs. Sugden was assisted in her business by her daughter, Mrs. Jackson, who brought up a large family there, some of whom may still live in the "Town upon the hill."

WINDY BANK.

"Last Sunday night aw went to Church,
And then went for a walk;
Aw met a curly-headed lad,
We had a cosy talk.
He had rosy cheeks, and teeth so white,
And eyes so blue and frank;
I'll tell you all about my lad,
He lives in Windy Bank.
Oh dear, say, can this be love?
He's neither learning, wealth, nor rank;
But I'll meet my bonny lad,
And he'll make my heart so glad,
The bonny lad that lives in Windy Bank."

We will now go to the top of Windy Bank. On the left stood the shop of Matthew Manley, flour and provision dealer. Opposite the Black Bull Inn, kept by a man called Smith, stood "Joe o' Ned's" stall, with black puddings, tripe, and trotters, steaming hot, and very good they were, too, on a winter's night. Then came Mr. Richmond's ironmonger's shop. He had one son, who married an actress, a play actor my mother used to call her. He had three sisters. Alice, a nice girl, married Captain Ayrton. I do not know whom Mary Ellen married. The youngest married her cousin, Frank Richmond, a partner in the firm. We will pass over Barnard Crook, cross the ginnell, and here is Bob Spencer, the tubber. His shop is filled with all kinds of toys, and baskets of all sorts and sizes. A little further down lived Mally and Jack Dugdale, a nice old couple. Mally went out nursing, and used to tell a funny story about her courting days. They had been walking out together for about six months, when one beautiful moonlight night they found themselves in Red Lane. Jack wanted Mally to sit down. Mally said "No," but thought there could be no harm in standing a few moments near the wall. Jack was murmuring those loving words that lovers love to hear, when Mally kissed him. Then, losing all control over himself, he threw his arms around her and cried, "Lass, Aw love thee so much, Aw could squeeze thee in two." Imagine their surprise when a couple of heads rose up behind the wall, and a voice cried, "All right, lad, squeeze her in two, and throw half over here." A second later Mally and Jack were flying helter-skelter down the road towards Colne. Mally used to say that thirty years after, whenever she thought about it, her heart bumped.

CHAPTER VI.

Quickly our pleasure glide away,
Our hearts recall the distant day,
  With many sighs;
The moments that are speeding past,
We heed not, but the past, the past
  More highly prize.

The next shop was a butcher's, kept by Hartley Metcalf; a little stout, jolly man he was, too. Then we came to the Bay Horse public-house; landlord's name, Harry Medlar. At the opposite corner stood the Masons' Arms public-house, which has long since lost its licence. The landlady of this house was a daughter of Mr. and Mrs. Nowell, who kept the Derby Arms Inn. I do not remember her married name. The Masons' Arms was a noted Colne hostelry from the early part of the 17th century. It was kept in 1760 by Christopher Edmondson and his wife. My own great-grandfather, my grandmother, Jenny Edmondson, married name Clitheroe, was born there in 1773. She used to say that she remembered the three sevens, 1777 very well. That is quite possible. I myself remember events that happened when I was six or seven years of age, while things that happened ten years ago have quite escaped my memory.

Christopher Edmondson had a family of three sons and four daughters. He appears to have prospered at the Masons' Arms, for as each girl married he made her a present of £100 as a start in life. That sum, small as it seems in our days of millionaires and the newly-rich, was considered then a nice little fortune. One of the daughters married, and kept the old coffee house on the opposite side. Another took a farm in the country. Another married and kept a general shop at the end of the buildings adjoining the new Red Lion Hotel. One of the sons, Christopher, was a baker and confectioner, and had a shop at the corner of Nineveh Street. Jane, another lass, was also a baker. Then came David — wild, adventure-loving David — who, in spite of his father's wishes and his mother's tears, enlisted for a soldier, fought at Waterloo, and came back, like the prodigal of old, to his home in dear old Colne upon the hill. But David was not the only one who went to fight for Old England in those troublesome days. No. There were many hundreds of bright young lads marching away day after day, and my grandmother told me that when Christopher and his young companions were tramping through the streets, with bands playing and colours flying, his mother stood amidst the crowd, weeping silently, and watching through her tears. They passed. The music of the band died in the distance. Then she turned, and, leaning heavily on her daughter's shoulders, cried, "They're somebody's lads. God look over them and spare them, and bring them safe home again."

Here, I cannot do better than quote from a stay-by, Willie Bell, entitled, "He fought at Waterloo," which appeared in the "Colne and Nelson Times" some time ago. It describes the return of the warriors of Colunio to the old town in 1815.

"Three years afterwards, tired of waiting and longing, heartsick and weary, news came of Wellington's great victory at Waterloo. The war was ended; there was joy throughout the land. The bells of the Old Church were set ringing, and bonfires were lighted on Pendle and Boulsworth, and all the range of the Cheviot Hills. When it was whispered that the Volunteers (those that were left, for, alas, some were sleeping their last sleep in an unknown grave) would soon be home again, Colne went wild with excitement, and determined to give her brave sons a right royal welcome. The hours sped on, and from every nook and window hung forth flags and bunting. The streets are alive with bright-faced, smiling people, for are not Colne's brave sons coming here to-day? Smiling matrons hurried from shop to shop in Market Street, carrying many little parcels. Little boys and girls in merry groups stood at the street corners, or hung on the railings, and the farmers, between their visits to the Angel and the Parkers' Arms, passed up and down the street, laughing and chatting. And now far away in the distance is heard the 'toot toot' of a horn. 'Hurrah; they come, they come,' cry the crowd. There is a rushing of feet, and a swaying of the multitude. A great lane is formed down the street. Then the roll of a drum falls upon the ears of the waiting crowds. Up in the Old Church belfry the old bells pealed and swaggered, and clanged out a greeting to the returning warriors. They were faintly answered by the clanging of another bell a mile away. The air was sweet and clear, as it always is in the old "Town on the Hill." 'Hurrah; they are in sight. See,' they cried, 'they come, they come.' And then a mighty shout of welcome went up from that waiting crowd as the 'Tally-ho' coach, with its load of travel-stained, battle-worn men, dashed up to the door of the Angel. There was silence for a moment. Then another mighty shout of welcome. Then such hand-shaking and kissing, such laughter and tears. 'My own lad, my first-born,' cries a mother, clasping a bronzed young fellow to her heart. 'Yes, mother,' he cries, 'home at last.'"

Well. This is the extract, and it gives a fair idea of one of the stirring scenes in the life of Colne in the old days; but it is sad to think that the waiting crowds, the warm, living, breathing, buoyant life, the flash and glitter of the uniforms, the blue of the sky overhead, the flowers, the endless stream of people, laughing,

chatting, merry-eyed, boisterous, well-fed, well-dressed —
this crowd that crushed so close to each other on that
day that they could almost feel the glad hearts beating
near to their own — it is sad to think that those voices are
hushed, those hearts are stilled, and the old town knows
them no more.

But to return to old Christopher Edmondson. At
the time of the opening of the Leeds and Liverpool
Canal, Christopher was one of the directors. There was
a great dinner given at Colne to all those interested in
the undertaking, and as a souvenir of the occasion a
number of black tobacco pots were made at the Leeds
pottery, and presented to each director. My mother
prized her grandfather's tobacco-pot greatly. It was at
home when I was married in 1862. I remember it well.
It was of black shiny ware, and round the jar in bas
relief were the figures of the 12 Disciples seated at the
Table of the Lord's Supper.

Christopher Edmondson's daughter, Mrs. Hirst, who
kept the general shop adjoining the New Red Lion, had
a family of four, two sons and two daughters. The sons
became ironmongers, and settled in Accrington. One
of the daughters died an old maid. Between you and
me, I think that is dreadful. Old maids are always dis-
appointing. They do not fulfil their mission in life, so
how can they be happy? Not they. Well, the
other daughter, Margaret Hirst, went as serving maid
to one of the Misses Ecroyd, of Edge End. She married
Mr. T. Ecroyd, and embraced the Quaker faith. They
travelled a great deal together. After going to the
cotton fields of America, and from there to the Cape of
Good Hope (the Kaffir land, my mother called it), they
returned to Edge End, firmly convinced that there was
no place in the world like "Home, sweet home." My
mother and Margaret were cousins, of course, and on
her return we were invited to Edge End. I remember
that visit as clearly as though it were yesterday, and
it is 60 years ago. We had dinner, and in the afternoon walked in the garden. When this sweet-faced
young Quakeress stooped to me and said, "Would'st

Church Street c.1890. On the right is a poster advertising the New Market Hall which opened in Dockray Street in 1898; in 1897 the market stalls were cleared from Colne's streets to relieve the congestion.

Church Street. On the right are the railings of the Wesleyan Chapel; opposite are a group of cottages known as Horsefield Fold, later the site of the Town Hall.

Church Street.

Looking down from Church Street into Westgate, on the left of the photograph stood the White Horse Inn which was demolished in 1886. Further down was the old King's Head, and across the road was the old Derby Arms.

thou like a posy?" I shyly said "Yes," and she gave me
a flower. We then inspected some curiosities brought
from abroad, and as the shades of night were falling,
when the shadows were filling the corners of the room,
and the moon was rising in the blue sky across the
fields, she sat down at the piano and began to play,
very soft and sweet at first, like dream music; then a
little louder and clearer, like distant bells; then she
sang that sweet old song,

> "Oh, the world seems sad and dreary
> Everywhere I roam,
> Oh, darkies, how my heart grows weary,
> All for the old folks at home."

The voice died away in almost a whisper. I turned
to my mother. She was sitting with her hands folded
in her lap, her face turned towards the sky, seen clearly
through the open window (for it was summer time), and
the tears were gently coursing down her cheeks. I went
up to her and said, "Mother, what's the matter?"
"Nothing, Jane," she answered. I wondered then why
my mother cried. I know now, for it is only when we
have passed through and known the passions of youth,
the trials of middle age, and entered on to the evening
of our lives, that we can look back and feel the beauty,
and the pathos, and hear the heart cry in the words,

> "Oh, darkies, how my heart grows weary,
> All for the old folks at home."

Now to return to the New Red Lion. It was kept by
the Asquith family for a great many years. Old Mr.
Asquith, grandfather to the postmaster, was Chief Con-
stable of Colne. My father, Thomas Ward, was a con-
stable of Colne, and, also, we had his staff of office (my
mother called it a cudgel). Don't laugh! It was painted
black, with "V. R." in gilt letters, and surmounted
by a crown. There was a number on it, which I have
forgotten. The last Asquith to keep the Red Lion was
Miss Sarah, who married Joseph Falshaw, who, with his
wife, became very popular in Colne, and lived there for
many years.

C

Dancing classes were held in a large club room over the bar of the New Red Lion 60 years ago. A Mr. Winder came from Manchester twice weekly and gave lessons. A guinea a quarter was the fee, and at the end of the term there was usually a dance given. This was called "The public day," when parents and guardians were allowed to come and see how their children were progressing. There was no tinkling piano to keep time. Mr. Winder taught us dancing quite in the old style. He danced and fiddled both at the same time, and it was wonderful what graceful dancers he made out of almost hopeless boys and girls in that dancing room at the Red Lion 60 years ago.

My sister, who was a pupil of Mr. Winder's, took me to one of the "Public day" balls. Miss Emmott-Green and her brother, from Emmott Hall, were there. They were called Emmott-Green then; now it is Green-Emmott. How is that, I wonder? Miss Emmott-Green was beautifully dressed, and wore her hair a-la-Marguerite in two long plaits, tied with brown ribbon. They drove away after the ball in a four-wheeled phaeton. I never saw them again. Soon after this they went on the Continent, and there was a sale at Emmott Hall. Another girl and I went, just to have a look at the old place. My father was amongst the people, and bought some red damask curtains.

The next corner shop was Mrs. John Norton's, pawnbroker. John Norton was the son of Mrs. Norton, the pawnbroker, I mentioned in a previous article. He had three little girls. His wife had just given birth to a fine baby boy when the father was taken ill and died in a few hours. I was taken in to see the new baby, and then into the next room where the father lay still in death. Mary Ann Norton and I were playfellows, and this happened while we lived near her grandmother, Mrs. Norton, in Windy Bank Top.

Next there were two private houses. Henry Bulcock, tailor and carpet-maker, lived in one, and Joseph Haighton in the other. Then there was, and still is, that good old house, the Angel Inn.

"And still she stands, clad in her daintiest robe,
The Angel greets the wanderers of the globe."
Here, I have heard my father say, the old stage
coaches put up in the old days. There was a very large
yard at the back, and a big dining room, used as a
dancing room, when my mother was a girl.

CHAPTER VII.

When Time, who steals our years away,
Shall steal our pleasures too;
The memory of the past will stay,
And half their joys renew.

Now we will return to the old coffee house on the
opposite side. Next to it was a very old-fashioned beer-
house, called "Dick of Anock's." The next was Chester's
tin shop, and Betty Emmerson, draper. Next was Mrs.
Gill's barber's shop. Of course she had a pole out.
Whoever knew a barber without one? Mrs. Gill's
daughter, Betsy, helped her mother to shave, and was
very clever at the business. Then William Asquith's,
chemist and druggist, brother to the postmaster. His
(William's) wife was just as hard working as himself.
They never had any children, and died worth plenty of
money. The next was Phillip's, ironmonger. Then we
come to Harry Hudder's shop. Harry was a flour
dealer, a nice quiet obliging man of the olden time. He
had two daughters, Margaret and Ann, who assisted
their father occasionally. The next was Oates Judson's
butcher's shop. Judson also had two daughters. One
married Robert Shaw, and the other, named Jane,
became the wife of Frank Hartley, of Dockray Square,
at one time clerk to Hartley and Carr, solicitors. The
next was Christopher Edmondson's confectioner's shop,
whom I have mentioned before. Then "Wolla" Whittaker's, silk hat manufacturer, whom I remember standing at his door, bowing and smiling to the people as
they passed. He used to have a beautiful white silk hat
on show in his window, similar to that worn by the last of

the dandies, Count D'Orsay. After "Wolla" Whittaker's
was Becca Halstead, a milliner. It was only a small
shop, but Becca had good taste. What she did she did
well. The next was a book shop, kept by a Mr. and
Mrs. Firth. Now we are right opposite the Angel Inn.
The next corner was a flour shop. I quite forget the
name, but the large house round the corner of Parlia-
ment Street was the home of Mr. Holroyd and daughters.
One married Mr. Lord, of Hartley and Lord, who rented
Walk Mill after we left it, and was the mother of Harry
Lord. The other corner of Parliament Street was Mr.
Banks', bread baker. I knew one of his daughters.
She married a Mr. Shackleton, joiner and undertaker,
Oxford Road, Burnley. She was one of Mrs. Black-
burn's scholars, and has died lately, and left a family.
Apropos of Mrs. Blackburn, her husband eloped with a
Mrs. Halstead, whose husband was killed in the Colne
riots, when the mob pulled down the Church railings
and charged the police. I ought, perhaps, to say con-
stables, as there were no police in Colne until after the
riots.

Next was a beer-house, kept by a man named Hartley.
Then at the top of Clayton Street was a superior looking
house, where lived a Mrs. Myers, formerly a Miss
Catherine Sagar, of Walk Mill. We will keep on this
side to the end of the walk and return to the Angel.
The next shop was kept by a man named Broadhurst,
gentleman's cap and tie provider. A hosier they call
that sort of place now. Mr. Broadhurst was tall and
thin, and had a couple of daughters, one quite a tall
girl and the other quite a dwarf. People said when
they went out together, "There's the long and the
short of it."

I wonder if the younger generation of Colne have any
idea of the fashions to be seen in Market and Church-
streets, and at Church 60 years ago. Well, the men
wore their hair much longer than now, and curled.
Young Ward, of Springwood House, gave my husband
a pair of curling tongs long before he was married. It
sounds silly and effeminate, doesn't it? But, on the

other hand, if one of the crop-eared young men of to-day had walked down Colne streets when I was a girl, people would have said he had just come out of prison. You have just to look at one of the portraits of our King, God bless him, to know how the hair was worn then. Wellington boots were also in fashion, and light trousers, with a black military-looking stripe running up the outside of the leg. Caps, now so universal, were only worn by pigeon flyers, dog fanciers, and prize fighters. As regards the ladies, the hair was worn piled high and drawn back from the forehead, after the fashion of the Empress Eugenie, then in the zenith of her beauty and splendour. This fashion afterwards developed into that abomination, the chignon. It was also worn in curls, piled high and falling in a sort of cascade down the back. It was about this time that the crinoline came up— another fashion set by the Empress—and obtained enormous dimensions. The dresses were wide and flounced, and with the crinoline underneath. I have actually seen pedestrians step into the gutter in Market Street and Church Street, to allow a lady to pass, and it was, of course, an impossibility to go through an ordinary doorway with any comfort or sense of security. I saw a stout old lady getting into her carriage outside the Church one Sunday. Her greatest difficulty was her crinoline. She took the hoops in one hand and got partly through the door, then made a dive for her seat. Alas, she stuck there, and up went the crinoline at the back, and, well, she'd a pair of cotton stockings on, as the song says. Now this little anecdote of the crinoline may seem an exaggeration to the young people of to-day, but here is an extract from a paper of the period 60 years ago :—

"The Crinoline Again.—In London two more lives have been sacrificed to that fashionable monster, the crinoline. A young lady, named Wegeth, was standing with her back to the fire, when a spark fell on her muslin dress, which was distended in the usual way by a crinoline, and in an instant she was enveloped in flames. She sustained dreadful injuries which ultimately resulted in death. The second case is of a

singular character. A woman was proceeding along
Camden Town when her foot became entangled in the
crinoline of a lady who was passing. She fell with great
violence, sustaining such severe injuries that she ex-
pired on the following morning."

Now a word in favour of the crinoline. By lifting
the dress away from the body, it allowed a woman freer
action of the limbs. Consequently, I think the women
of an older generation walked better than they do in
the clinging skirts of to-day.

But to return to our chat about old Colners. After
Broadhurst's was Petty, the stay maker and tailor. Mrs.
Petty was the stay maker of Colne, as Mrs. Caton is
of Burnley to-day. Now we cross St. John-street. At
the other corner was a fancy pot shop kept by a Mr.
and Mrs. Thornber. Next was Robinson, the butcher,
then a grocery store, and at the top of Railway-street,
just round the corner, was Cockshutt, the tallow chand-
ler. They did a large business in those days. The
other girls and I, as we came from school, used to watch
them making candles through the cellar gratings. But
stay, what is this? A funeral. Slowly the sombre
procession winds its way down the street. Sable plumes,
heavy bands and wreaths of crepe, and all the parapher-
nalia of woe. But who are those two mourners, who,
with bended heads and solemn visage, follow in its wake?
Need I ask? No, I remember you; poor, harmless old
Billy and Jack Crawshaw—remember you because people
said you were both "nobbut tenpence to t' shilling."
You followed many an old friend to their last resting
place. You, too, are laid side by side, near those who
have gone before. But there are still those in the "Town
on the Hill" who remember you still. Another well-
known character of Colne sixty years ago was Harry
Bracewell, the watchman. I remember looking from
my bedroom window at night, when on the stillness would
break the steady tramp of the night watchman as he
moved leisurely down the street, muffled up in his long
overcoat, ready on the least provocation to spring his
rattle, and crying "Two o'clock and a fine morning."

Then there was old Binns, who used to bring the water for people from the old well that supplied Colne Hall with water in those days. Oh, I can smile even now at the recollection of his well-known figure, with a tub of water on his head and a can in either hand, which he would carry safely home without spilling a drop, a feat which no other person in Colne could perform.

After Cockshutt's were a few more shops. In one lived a Miss Ingham, a dressmaker. Miss Ingham was fair, fat, and over fifty. One day the carriage from Alkincoates drove up with a lady visitor who wanted a dress making by a certain date, the event being a bazaar in aid of the Church. It was "Dear this," and "Dear the other" to old Miss Ingham, until the old lady, as she said afterwards, scarcely knew whether she was on her head or her heels. The time was fixed for the fitting-on, and the dress was to be ready for the bazaar. The lady drove up to Miss Ingham's the day before the great event, and was disappointed to find the dress not ready. However, she was, as before, all honey, and then Miss Ingham told her how busy she had been, and how tired she was, but she would have the dress ready before the time. The lady said, "You will? Oh, it is good of you, dear. I shall never forget you. Good-bye, dear, don't forget." She went out. The carriage door was held open by a gentleman for the lady to enter. "Is it not ready?" he asked. "No," snapped the lady, "the old cat says she has been too busy." Miss Ingham afterwards said she would have given something to have her inside her shop for five minutes with the door shut. So would I.

CHAPTER VIII.

I hear your well-loved voices, friends,
    O'er all the years gone by;
Oh, how my heart rejoices, friends,
    But, oh, I want to cry.

Over the shops occupied by Miss Ingham and others at that time was a large warehouse belonging to "Tom-o'-

Bob's," and Critchley and Armstrong, cotton brokers, Colne and Manchester, also had offices there. Watson Bracewell was bookkeeper for them, and he married a Miss Elizabeth Walker, milliner and dressmaker, and had a family. My father was a great friend of them all. When we removed from Walk Mill to the top of Windy Bank he gave our large Newfoundland dog to Mr. Critchley, who took it to Manchester. One day, two or three years after, my father was talking to some friends in Church Street when Lion bounced up to him and with both paws on his shoulders tried to lick his face. Startled, his friends stepped back, but Lion was too delighted to hurt his old master. Then he bounded off. My mother was in the shop when the old dog, whose back was as high as the counter, dashed in, and how delighted she was to see him. How he found us out we never knew, but some time afterwards Mr. Critchley arrived in Colne and took Lion away; we never saw him again. It is sweet to remember even the affection of a dog, and how true and faithful they are to those who are kind to them. I believe it was Gordon Stables, the famous author, who, when asked one day if he thought dogs went to heaven, said: "Well, I don't know; but I think I should not like to go if Lassie was not there." Lassie is the name of a dog that had been his constant companion for years. I, too, have a dog, named Gladis. Gladis is not as famous as Lassie, but she is just as affectionate and true. Do you know, I really believe my little dog knows when I am not well or in trouble, for she sleeps on a chair at the side of my bed, and when I am thinking sometimes I look down and see her wistfully looking up at me, as much as to say: "I know you are downhearted, but cheer up, it will all come right in the end"; and then she will pat my knee with her paw. Ah, well! that is what we all hope for, that it will all come right in the end, and it will. God will see to that.

Now we have got to where the old Toll Bar used to stand, right opposite the third house before you get to the Baptist Chapel. This was kept by a man named Capstick. Here, as a girl, with my companions, I have

Mr. Robert Shaw, J.P., Senr.

Mr. Robert Shaw, J.P., Junr.

Mr. Thomas Thornber England, J.P.

Mr. W. C. Asquith,
For several years Chairman of the old Colne Local Board.

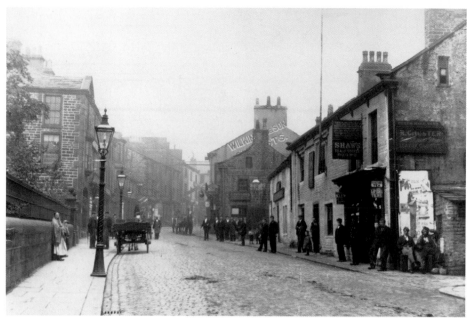

Church Street after 1875 without the cattle and market stalls. On the right are the Fleece and the Parkers Arms. A typical Victorian street scene with gas lamps, paved walkways and cobbled setts in the road. Gas was introduced to Colne in 1839; one of the first gas explosions in the town occurred in 1896, a house suffering a great deal of structural damage but human casualties were slight – the tenant had his spectacles blown off, a horse was frightened and a PC startled.

Church Street, with J Spencer's Tea and Coffe Rooms on the left.

stood and watched the lime "gals.," about 30 of them (they were small shaggy horses), with rough wooden saddles on their backs, and over the saddles were hung a couple of sacks and boxes filled with lime from Lothersdale in the morning, and returning in the evening loaded with coal and other things. Bells were hung from the horses' necks, and tinkled musically on the summer air. As they passed us, led by the red-faced lads and men, we used to sing:

> Bell-horses, bell horses,
> What time o' day?
> One o'clock, two o'clock,
> Off and away.

Now we will go as far as Carry Lane Head, and return to the Angel Inn, where we left off. The houses on the right were then new ones. A Mr. Joe Smith lived in the first. and had a family of girls, whom I knew; in the next lived Lawyer and Mrs. Hartley and her mother, Mrs. Manknowles. Those ladies dressed beautifully, as did all the better class of Colne then. So you will understand the attraction for us children at the church gates even in winter, for the ladies then wore a great deal of ermine and fur, a fashion set, I believe, by the late Queen Victoria. God bless her, who knew better than anyone what made a plain face attractive and a beautiful face more beautiful still. In the next block lived Dr. Ayre, and Mr. George and Miss Fidelia Carr. Then we came to the house of Sam Catlow, father of young Sam Catlow, who was then only a boy, but who was destined to become the first Mayor of Colne. I knew him and his sister, Sarah Ann, and a brother John; the younger branches of the family I did not know.

Now across the road, opposite the Carrs, stood, and still stands, I think, the old Carry Lane Head House, tenanted when I was a girl by Dr. Henry Buck and his sister, who, I believe, kept house for him. What a quaint old-world house it seemed to me, with its old-fashioned doorway and circular steps! There must be an interesting history connected with this old house;

will anyone oblige? The next house is, I should say, almost as old, and is next to the Angel. Mr. Waddington Hartley lived here. Next was a cottage in which lived John Binns, licensed auctioneer and sale crier. The word "sale crier" is obsolete—cheap printing has killed it; but John Binns used to gather a crowd by ringing a bell, then announce the sale, and of course when his voice was heard there was a rush from all directions. Now across the road, and side by side almost, lived Mr. Richmond and Captain Aireton, Mr. Midgely, silk hat manufacturer, whose works were at the bottom of Windy Bank. Then the chapel, after that the row of houses where stood Mrs. Blackburn's dear old school. How can I pass it, the place where I and so many of Colne's daughters have spent so many happy hours, hours which, alas, we ne'er can know again!

For there, with friends far sundered,
  I roved in glee lang syne,
And never foot was lighter yet
  On Colne's old hill than mine,
And with such shouts of gladness
  We startled hill and plain,
I'd give a year of all things here
  To raise the like again.

But though my feet have wandered,
  This heart will e'er be true,
And many a weary heart like mine
  Would fain be there "the noo."
And many a dear old Colneite
  Like me full often prays
That yon murmuring rills on Colne's fair hill
  May see his sunniest days.

Now we are at Dyson New Road, as it was called then, now Skipton Road. But what a change is here! Look at those rows of houses, stretching as far as the eye can reach! Then there were hedges and fields on either side, and right down you could just see at the bend of the road Dick Lambert's size-house, the only building on the road. Dick had only one hand; the other had been lost through an accident at his work. My father and he were friends. He was married and had a family. One of his daughters married Henry Ward, a tea dealer, and lived in a house built by her father next to the size-house. They had a son who became a well-known Burnley tradesman, Mr. Ward, ironmonger, of St. James' Street. Beyond the size-house the white road stretched away amidst fields and trees, dotted here and there with cottages, and far away in the distance Old Pendle stood solemn, grand, and majestic, the highest and most famous of all the hills around. I used to wonder as a child what there could be on the other side of it, and used to dream of some day getting on the top and looking down; it seemed to my childish imagination to be the end of the world. I wonder if anyone will, some of these days, write all the stories and tales of Colne country-side. My father, who was born in 1800, used to point to a stone in a field below the size-house on which a sheep-stealer had been hanged. It happened this way: he had at night crept to the field, caught the sheep, and, tying it with ropes, slung it over his back. At the edge of the field he rested the sheep on the stone for a few moments the sheep slipped down the other side of the stone, the rope tightened round the man's neck, and he was found the next morning dead. When we were children we hurried past that field at night, fearful lest we should see the ghost of the sheep-stealer. Then there is the legend of the building of the Old Church that my grandmother used to tell us children. It seems that they commenced to build the old church at Kirk Clough, but as soon as it was built in the day, it was, by some mysterious agency, pulled down at night. So the monks—those jolly, red-faced old chaps we see in old pictures—determined to watch, and one beautiful moonlight night they hid themselves in the bushes round the partly-built church. They waited; and presently from under the branches of an old oak a little green man walked out, followed by a beautiful fairy queen, whose crown of diamonds shed a blue light around. They were followed by scores of other little green men, who set to work, and soon there was not one stone left on the top of another. The monks rushed out furiously from their hiding place. The leader and his little green men vanished with a burst of elfin laughter, and as the fairy queen faded away she sang:

This church will ne'er be built aright;
Up in the day, down in the night.
Build it upon old Colne hill,
And at the Judgment Day 'twill be there still.

And there it was built, and there it has stood through all the ages; firm as the rock of the Empire, and dear to the heart of Colne as liberty itself.

But here we are at the chapel, which was not exactly a chapel but a sort of Mechanics' Institute. Next was Hartley Parkinson's, wine and spirit merchant, whose daughter, Miss Parkinson, married Mr. Lazarus Threlfall. They had three sons, Richard, Hartley, and Joseph. Now we come to Clark, the clogger, and Brunton, at the corner of Dockray Square. There was a Ward, tea dealer, here, also Mark Lund, who lived in a private house, but had a stall at his door on which he always had a fine show of apples and oranges. I think he must be dead; it is years since I saw his kind, genial face over the stall.

Now we have walked from the Craven Hotel to Carry Lane Head, through the town on both sides, right and left. The health of the people of Colne must have been very good in my time. They did not require many doctors, and, you know, a demand creates a supply; but the doctors of Colne could be counted on the fingers of one hand 60 years ago. There was Dr. Buck, and his two sons, Dr. Henry and Dr. Edward Buck, Dr. Ayre and one assistant, Dr. Cockroft and Dr. Doyle. Now Dr. Ayre used to ride up to Marsden Hall every morning, wet or fine, to see the Misses Walton and their brother, as long as they lived. How well I remember him jogging along on his old brown horse. My mother (who was sometimes short of what Betty Booth called "the root of all evil,") used to say, "There goes Dr. Ayre. I'll bet he's earned another 5s.; I wish he'd come and spend it on cakes." Now we'll have a walk down Colne Lane. There were some very nice houses; then the Cross Keys was kept by a man named Crawshaw, father of the two lads, "Billie" and Jack Crawshaw, whose weakness it was to follow all the funerals. The next was a fine house where some of the officers lived when the soldiers were in the barracks at the old Cloth Hall—but I'll tell you more about that another time. The next was Messrs. Holmes, solicitors, of Hardacre. Now on the opposite side, on the left, there used to be a funny-looking place with arched doors and windows. It was called "The Dungeon" or "Old Lock-up." Then there was a fold, or yard, with three or four houses, and a shoeing forge and smithy. The smith's name was Rycroft. The youths of Colne went there to have irons put on their clogs. Now a little further down we come to a house with two windows; one window was filled with cakes and fruits, the other with tinware. This was the home of Pickles Hartley—now Sir William Hartley. His mother, a pleasant woman, always had a kind word for whoever entered her shop.

CHAPTER IX.

Jog on, jog on, the footpath way,
  And merrily hunt the stilia;
The merry heart goes all the day,
  Your sad tires in a mile-a.

And that's true. So we'll jog on past the boyhood's home of the "Knight of Colne," and come to Samuel Smith, the skinner, or fellmonger. Further on was Sarah Brown's grocery shop. Everybody knew Sarah, and, what is more, liked her. She was the mother of the late Robert Brown, of the Borough Saw Mills, Burnley, another "captain of industry," of whom old Colne might well be proud. Robert Brown's son was, a few years ago, the landlord of the Hall Inn, Burnley.

I believe he is now in America, and doing well. A little lower down was the house of Mr. Robert Shaw, adjoining the mill. Now let us stroll on, over Greenfields, to Walton's farm-house and barn. Then we come to Pickles' draper's shop on one side, and Ayrton's woollen warehouse on the other. Pickles, the draper, 60 years ago, did a great business with all the best people round Colne country-side. It used to be said I think if that sack of coppers was there to-day we cellar below the shop which they had not time to count. I think if that sack of coppers was there to-day we could find a few people to help them. The Pickles were four in family, two brothers and two sisters—Henry and William, and Mary Ann, and I think the other sister's name was Alice. Their parents, the founders of the business, were dead long before my time. Henry was the buyer, and went to Manchester, Liverpool, and other large centres for goods. William and the two sisters, with a couple of assistants, served behind the counter. The Misses Pickles were nice girls, with pale golden hair, worn parted in the centre. There were no fringes over the forehead then; when they did come up they were treated with ridicule and called "donkey fringes." I believe it was our own sweet Queen-Mother who first made them popular. The Misses Pickles had the knack of at once making one feel at home as soon as you entered their shop. There was always the smile, and a word of greeting; and patience in finding you whatever you wanted. Patience and politeness; that is the secret of success in business. How I wish some of those young damsels in our post-offices would be a little more obliging. Some of them serve you with such a "languid-oh-don't-hurry-me-please" kind of air, as much as to say, "Oh, I'm really not compelled to be here, don't you know," and, after the exertion of handing you a penny stamp, they look as if they were going to faint. What sort of housewives they will make, when the time comes, I don't know, nor do I want to know. But the Misses Pickles were ladies in the highest sense of the word, and they prospered, as they deserved. On Wednesdays, market days, the shop was packed all day, and cart-loads of goods were taken away. Henry

Pickles died very wealthy. The names of the assistants were Joseph Heys and John Ridehalgh (a bonny, curly-headed lad, whom I knew). The last time I saw him, after the lapse of years, I was shocked, so great was the change. He, too, is gone, and, like so many of the people of these "Memories," returns but in our dreams.

Now we will go down the Waterside. Here stood the old Buck Spout, the water of which was always so clear and cold. There was a tradition among the old women that the Buck Spout water ("'t' water," the old dames used to call it) made the best tea. Once, as a girl, I went with my mother to call on a friend of my grandmother's, then nearly 80 years of age. As though it were yesterday, I can see her standing there in her winsey gown and check apron. I see again the smile of greeting, and hear her voice, saying, "Come thy ways in, an' sit thee daan, an' awl fotch a tin full of water frae t' Buck Spout, an' we'll hae a dish o' tay an' a tay cake, an' a drop o' t' owd craythur frae t' Robin Hood." Well, a drop of the "old craythur" was brought, and they sat and talked of things that happened long before I was born, and I sat there, fascinated and silent, listening to it all. Talking of the Robin Hood, there used to be a sign over the door with the name of the landlord, and a large picture painted in oils—and very well painted, too—of the famous archer, in all the glory of green doublet and hose, surrounded by his merry men, while Friar Tuck leaned, in a state of collapse, against a tree. Robin himself was letting an arrow fly at a stag which, standing some distance away, watched him calmly out of the corner of his eye, as much as to say "Go on; you can't shoot for nuts." Maid Marian was not in evidence; perhaps she had gone home, and been soundly "spanked" for running after the gallant archer. Another famous Waterside public-house was the Old Duke Inn. It was on the Green, opposite where the "Charity Sermons" were preached on Sundays; and against the wall, at the side of the Old Duke, seats were erected, on which the school children sat, tier above tier. Ah, me, I can see them now; their sweet angel faces untouched by the cares and troubles of life, and their voices raised in

childish supplication to their own True Shepherd in
Heaven. Where are they all now, I wonder? Gone;
each their separate ways. Some may be resting on
Colne hillside, and some may have been tempted out
into the great world, and have fallen by the way.

Oh, happy days of childhood;
Oh, souls without a stain.
Oh, summer flowers; oh, dear dead hours;
Lost days recalled in vain.

It was here that the Rushbearing took place. The
Rushbearing was, I believe, originally a ceremonial of
the Church; but someone who knows more about it than
I will, no doubt, explain. It was a sort of feast, or
country fare in my time, and was held on the Green,
which was covered with swinging boats and round-
about, toffee and nuts, and gingerbread stalls. Oh,
that gingerbread! It makes my mouth water even now;
and the gold on it. Why, there was as much gold as
ginger. Ah, those were merry gatherings, because
those old-world customs have a charm all their own.
The Rushbearing brought a lot of country lads and lasses
into the town. It was a time for social re-union, and
for an exchange of courtesies that had a genuine, old
English flavour about them that was delightful to all.

There was another public-house down the Waterside.
I do not remember the sign of it, but the landlord's
name was Rushton. It stood right opposite the
Old Duke, at the corner of the Square. I remember
Mr. Harry Sunderland, who was a travelling draper,
and his three daughters (Annie, Emily, and Amelia).
Then there was Holmes, the grocer, just at the corner,
near the old Peel Laithe Farm, which was pulled down
to make room for a factory at the bottom of Blascomay.
The last farmer to farm Peel Laithe Farm was John
Atkinson, jovial, red-faced, merry John Atkinson. All
the meadows in the flat belonging to the farm were taken
by my father, when John gave up, and joined to Colne
Hall Farm, and it was on the bottom meadow, opposite
the mill dam, where the first mowing machine that ever
came into Colne was tried for the first time. It was

Mrs Edmundson's millinery shop at 34 Market Street.

The toll bar at the top of Skipton Road was part of the Blackburn, Adingham and Cocking End Turnpike. It reached Colne in 1804, extending to Lidgett in 1810.

Angel Inn Market Street, built in 1770. A large inn with stabling space, it was a coaching inn serving the Invincible coaches, and therefore much in demand for all sorts of public functions. Dances were held in the huge dining room in the 1830s. A stone angel that stood on a shelf just inside the door disappeared in the 1930s.

Colne Lane was once part of the main transport route through Colne when the roads ran from Windy Bank and down Colne Lane into Waterside and over the hills into Yorkshire. This part of Colne was the home to many professional people: Dr. Ayre, John Conyers the registrar for Colne and Joshua Duckworth at Caxton House. The Mansion House on Burrens Meadow was once owned by the influential Midgeley family. In 1789 a fearful storm hit Colne and a George Aspden perished in the snow down Colne Lane – a verdict of 'accidental death' was recorded. From the top of Colne Lane the Colne Girls' Race was held and whoever reached the Commercial Hotel first would receive a dress length.

considered a wonderful invention, and crowds of people, not only farmers, but shop-keepers, came from far and near to see it worked. It was bought by Mr. Shaw for his farm at Trawden.

CHAPTER X.

Now, let us take a walk up Colne Hall fields, round by the well, up the well-worn steps, and out into Albert Road, to Spring Lane top. where our house stood. Every house has a history; some sad, some merry, some pathetic. I will tell you of the building of ours, for every stone of that house at the top of Spring Lane was paid for by a loving mother, who worked her fingers to the bone that it might be shared amongst her children. Ah, and watered by a mother's tears! Now, for some time things had not been as prosperous with us as my father and mother would have liked; for, although we farmed Colne Hall Farm, we lived at the top of Windy Bank, and, to make matters worse, just at this time we received notice to quit our house in three months. My mother was heart-broken. "Troubles never come singly," she said, brokenly. My father said, "Well, cheer up, we'll manage to pull through, lass. It shall never be said to my children that I became a bankrupt or did a shabby trick by my fellow-men." As it happened, my father had shares in the Waterside Building Society, and he and my brother went to see Mr. Statter, the land agent for the Earl of Derby. So, as we were already tenants under him on Colne Hall Farm, the spot chosen to build a house on was Spring Lane top, close to, and opposite the old barn. Now, to get the house built and ready in short of three months was a puzzler, as my mother used to say. So we all put our shoulders to the wheel. We had, of course, horses and carts of our own, so my brothers brought lime from Lothersdale, and the men began to dig the foundations. Stone was brought from Catlow Delph, and some from Noyna Delph. Even my mother helped when she could, and my brother Jonathan and I, when we came home from school, riddled the sand while father shovelled it

D

into the riddle, to save a man's wage. The weeks sped
on, the walls rose higher and higher. Oh, how anxiously
those dear ones, now at rest near the Church, watched
them as they rose. Sometimes Jonathan and I, child-
like, rebelled at having to work instead of play, but my
father would say, "Come on and help; whatever there
is shall be shared amongst you some day, for this house
is our own." One's own! What fascination there is
in the word, even to a child! But it was never shared.
When my father died his will was written, but never
signed. It was brought to him just as the breath left
his body. "Well, what shall we do, mother," I said,
"if the house is not ready in time?" "Oh," she
replied, "we'll go in if the walls are there and the roof
on." Well, the walls were up, and the roof was on, but
that was all, when the three months came to an end;
so, after closing time on the Saturday, we set to work,
and by the early hours of the Sunday morning we had
everything into our new house. If we had remained
in the old home until Monday we should have entered
on another quarter, and that my father wished to avoid.
I remember that flitting so well. How we all worked,
and how we laughed because there were no steps into
the house, and we had to walk on planks to get in. And,
as the May sunshine flooded the unplastered walls of
that kitchen, we all sat down to breakfast, tired out,
but with thankful hearts. And my poor mother said,
with tears in her eyes, "Thank God, we are under our
own roof at last. No one can put us out." My father
rose, his heart too full for words, and, leaning over the
table, gently kissed my mother. I saw the love and
trust in his eyes as he did so. This house we built was
the only one at the top of Spring Lane at that time.
It is the one on the left as you go down the Lane. It
has a side door and steps outside, with railings leading
to the cellar kitchen. But, although we had our own
house, it had to be paid for at the rate of £4 per month.
It was this anxiety and work to pay this that helped
to shorten my mother's days. She had no spare cash
to pay for nurses, night or day, and was literally—like
our dear dead King—working to the end. She died
peacefully, sitting in her chair one Sunday, after

dinner, quietly and serenely, like all the children of God who are tired with their burden, and welcome rest.

When all the world is young, lad,
And all the trees are green,
And every goose a swan, lad,
And every lass a queen;
Then hey for boot and spur, lad,
And round the world away,
Young blood must have its course, lad,
And every dog its day.

When all the world is old, lad,
And all the trees are brown,
And all the sport is stale, lad,
And all the wheels run down;
Creep home and take your place there,
The spent and maimed among,
God grant you find one face there
You loved when all was young.

C. Kingsley.

And I shall creep home some day to that dear old "Town upon the Hill," and I thank God, from my heart, that there are a few faces left whom I loved when I was young; and if they, too, should pass over to the "great beyond" before I come, well, I can at least find the rest everlasting beside them, can't I?

Next to our house in Spring Lane were two cottages built by us. In one of them lived a Mr. and Mrs. Stansfield. Mrs. Stansfield was an old lady, much older than her husband, who was, nevertheless, much devoted to her. She was aunt to Mrs. Hallam, of Marsden Hall, and was reputed wealthy. It seems to me that in those days people were not what you might call house-proud. They were content to live in a small way, without show, and not with so much ostentation as now. At any rate, the Stansfields were very comfortable in our cottage, for, when I took the milk at 8 o'clock in the morning, Mr. Stansfield would be up and have the fire lighted, the table laid for breakfast, and his wife's slippers airing in front of the fire. My mother, who popped in herself sometimes with the milk, said how comfortable they were, and what a good husband he seemed to be. Not that my own father was not a good husband, but there are some men who understand and give those little attentions to women which are so much appreciated. Mr. Stansfield was one of them. He helped his wife with the housework; in fact, he did most of it for her. About noon on fine days they would be dressed, and take their walks abroad, visiting Mrs. Hallam, at Marsden Hall, and other well-known people. Mrs. Stansfield died rather suddenly, and Mr. Stansfield found himself with a nice competence. He still lived in our cottage, and what do you think? He paid his addresses to his wife's niece, Mrs. Hallam, of Marsden Hall (went coortin', the gossips called it), was accepted, and the man who lived in our cottage and did his own housework drove his carriage through the streets of Colne. But prosperity did not spoil him, for if kindness and simplicity can make a gentleman, he was one. Some years afterwards I was at Blackpool, when who should I see coming along the front but Mr. and Mrs. Stansfield? He recognised me, and, smiling, turned to his wife and said, "This is our little milkmaid." She shook hands with me, and hoped I should enjoy my visit, and I believe the second marriage was as happy as the first. Talking of marriage, I do not believe that all women marry for a husband in the accepted sense of the word, as much as for companionship, and the sense of security a man in the house gives one. To give you an instance:—

When I was a little girl, there lived in a large house, between Nelson and Colne, nearer Nelson than Colne, three maiden ladies. They kept a nice establishment; a cook and housemaid, a kitchen-maid, a coachman, who was married, and a butler, named James ————. The butler, who had been taken by the father of the ladies when a lad to ride out with them on their ponies and look after them, had spent his whole life in their service. He had followed his master and mistress to their graves, and had wept with their daughters, as though

he mourned a dearly-loved parent of his own. The
years rolled on, and age came almost before they
realised that middle-age was past. James was with
them still, and, through all the years, had given them
the same ungrudgingly faithful service as of old. Is it
any wonder that they relied upon him as one of themselves, and that James gave these three old ladies, with
all their wealth, that sense of security that women like
to feel in the companionship of a man? So you can
imagine their distress and consternation when James
(who had been left a legacy) came to them and said he
would like to leave. They said very little at first; the
blow seemed to them too great to be true; but they
cried quietly together that night. James to go; oh, it
could not be thought of! For nearly 40 years he had
been, not their servant, but their friend. Oh, just like
an elder brother. Oh, anything rather than be left
alone. So they dried their tears, and hit on a plan.
James must not go; one of them would marry him. It
did not matter which he chose, as long as he remained
as guide, philosopher and friend The next night, after
dinner, the bell rang, and when James entered the
dining room he found his three ladies sitting in their
black silk and lace dinner dresses, a trifle agitated, their
faces bearing traces of tears, but outwardly calm. This
was long before the time of George Lashwood's song,
"Three women for every man," or you might imagine
them rising as James entered and singing,

> Oh, James,
> There's three women for every man,
> Now, James, say, if you can,
> Why shouldn't every man
> Have three wives?

But, no. As James entered the room, the elder came
forward and said: "James, we cannot bear the idea of
your leaving us. Except for you we are alone in the
world, so, if you will stay with us, one of us will marry
you. We do not mind which you choose, as long as
you stay." Well, mam," said James, stolidly as ever,
"I think I'll take Miss Jane." (Miss Jane was the

youngest; not a bad judge, James). "I am quite willing, James," said Miss Jane, and went over and put her hand in his. It is to be hoped that James showed a little affection and kissed her. However, they were married and were very happy. So this proves that it is companionship a woman wants, doesn't it?·

CHAPTER XI.

But how changed the scene down Spring Lane to-day to what it was 60 years ago! Now there are rows upon rows of streets. Then, there were a few paltry cottages which ran down the right side to the bottom. Down the left side were gardens belonging to the cottages, and over the gardens the green fields and the landscape around. In one of the cottages lived Mr. John Walker, who was manager at Vivary Bridge Mill, owned by a Mrs. Thornber, who was a widow, with two children, boy and girl. I do not think that in all my experience I ever saw a woman as stout as Mrs. Thornber. It was simply impossible for her to walk far. In fact, I do not remember seeing her outside the garden gate of the house by the mill, only when she was driven out by old Bob Rushton in the trap. Bob helped in the garden and pottered about the house, doing odd jobs for the maid of all work. They say "laugh and grow fat." The least thing set Mrs. Thornber laughing, when she shook all over like a jelly. The people who tenanted the cottages in Spring Lane were all industrious, hard-working people. One family were heald knitters, in another cottage a man kept a shop and sold blacking which he made himself. It had a certain reputation for the gloss it gave the factory lasses' clogs, and was in great demand. His name was Dobson. On Fridays and Saturdays he hawked his blacking, and on Sundays (he was a local preacher) he used to pass our house on his way to a chapel at Blacko, to preach. Then, of course, he was dressed in black cloth and white choker (my mother called white ties chokers), his boots reflecting the rays of the sun with his own blacking, which my

brother swore he used for his silk hat also, it was so
glossy. Then there were the Bracewells, who owned
and lived in their own house, painters and decorators.
The two Misses Bracewell were quite superior young
women. In another cottage lived Tom Croasdale, who
was the first railway porter to wear a uniform in Colne
after the opening of the railway. A great many of the
people living in the houses worked at Thornber's Mill.
In another cottage lived Robert Briggs, a shoemaker,
and his wife, Dolly Briggs. They farmed a small piece
of land near the bottom of Spring Lane, called jokingly
by the neighbours "the halfpenny cake," it was so small.
They had one cow which nibbled the grass of the puny
"cake," and gazed mournfully over the hedge at the
people as they passed. Talking of cows, although we
farmed Colne Hall Farm, I only tried once to milk a
cow, but, never again. It was all through my brother
Edmondson, who seemed to think we none of us did
enough for the place. It was this way. John had gone
to Burnley, and Edmondson said to my mother, "Why
can't our Jane milk to-night?" "Why, she has never
learnt," said my mother. "No, and she never will if
she doesn't try," said he. So my mother said, "Well,
Jane, go and try what tha can do." So I got my milk-
ing pail and stool and sat down near one of our cows we
called Nellie. I drew the milk once or twice, but they
know as well as anyone if any strange hand touches
them. So Nellie kicked out, and round came her tail
across my eyes; over went the stool, and for a moment
I tried desperately to balance myself on my head, but
failed, not being used to that position. Then I scuttled
out of the shippon and ran home, thinking I was done
for. My mother told Edmondson that she would not
have us girls, Mary or I, doing their work. We were
never asked again. But to return to the Briggs. They
had a family. John, one son, went to Bolton and established a coal and coke business there, and, I believe,
did well. Dina Briggs married twice, and is now a
widow. Now we will go through the beautiful Church
Meadows, through Turney Crook, where lived Harry
Simpson, the bellman, and into Windy Bank.

At eventide I stumbling struck the case
That held my light guitar,
And notes like long lost voices filled the space,
Faint, faint, as from afar.

Through Turney Crook into Windy Bank. In
Turney Crook on the left lived Harry Simpson, the bellman, a well-known Colne character. He was a shoemaker by trade, had a pleasant little woman for a wife,
and a son, Mitton Simpson, who was a tailor. If a
child was lost, or a bazaar or sale to be held, Harry
went round Colne and announced it. Til-ling, til-ling,
til-ling, went his bell, when of course, there was a rush
from all directions. On the right-hand corner of
Turney Crook stood the Walton Arms, a very old house,
belonging to the Waltons, of Marsden Hall. It was
on the death of the Misses Walton, of Marsden, that
Mrs. Hallam, who married Mr. Stansfield, succeeded
to the property. Miss Hallam was a girl about my
own age, and was driven to Colne almost every day by
old George Cocks, the coachman, who was left a pound
a week by the late owners. There were no municipal
buildings then, and Mr. Ainsworth, the relieving officer,
had rooms at the Walton Arms, where he saw people
and transacted business; but I think he and his family
lived at Padiham. Now right on the opposite side were
two beer-houses. One was kept by Peter Nowell. The
other was called the Jovial Hatters. The name came
from the silk hat industry, which was a flourishing trade
in Colne at one time. There was a young man who,
from his apprenticeship days, wore nothing else, and
was called by old Colners, "The Swell Hatter." The
next was Hargreaves Hudson's pot shop, attended to by
his wife and family, while Hargreaves himself was a
painter and decorator. One of his daughters married
a Mr. Charles Tatham. Martha, the youngest, and I
were true friends until they left Colne for Leeds, when
I lost sight of them. Some years afterwards I was
coming down Albert Road when I saw a lady in widow's
weeds, whose face seemed familiar. As she came nearer
I saw it was my old friend, Martha, but how changed
from the merry girl I had known in the past! She gave

Mr. William Ayrton.   Mr. Thomas Charnley.

Colne Lane: beyond the tree was Caxton House, home of Joshua Duckworth, one of three well known brothers; Francis Duckworth who wrote the hymn tune 'Rimington', Caleb Duckworth who was apprenticed to William Pickles Hartley and then went on to run his own business from Victoria Mill, Colne Lane, and Joshua who set up his own printing business and was responsible for opening probably the first purpose-built cinema in the country, Central Hall on Colne Lane. Before the age of cars it was still safe for the young children to play on the road with their home made wooden toys.

Robin Hood Inn Waterside also known as the 'Robin Hood and Little John' appeared about 1824. The first landlord was John Whitaker and its longest serving was Robert Tillotson 1883-98.

The Admiral Lord Rodney named after the admiral who saved the West Indies from French attack in 1782, overlooked Mill Green where the rush bearing and Wapping Pash events took place. At the Wapping Pash there were huge potato pies, ginger bread stalls, coconut shies and donkey rides.

me her card and warmly pressed me to call. I never
saw her again. Next lived William Holt, the daily
carrier from Colne to Burnley, a pleasant man who died
suddenly and left a wife and large family. So Mrs.
Holt, the brave woman, kept the business on herself
along with her eldest son, a lad of 12 or 14, and brought
her family up a credit to the town. Further down was
a confectioner's and toffee shop. They sold some delightful sweets that we called cherries and berries. I
used to watch them through the shop window pour the
hot stuff from a pan into a funny-looking machine, and
they dropped down like glass balls into a tray. Then
there was a beer-house called "Live and let live." Not
a bad sign for a pub., is it? It stood at the corner of
a street called High Street. At the other corner, on
the left, was one called "Speed the Plough." The landlord's name was Tom Clark. Further down I do not
remember much until we come to Cabbage Lane. There
stood a good house, where Mr. and Mrs. Smith, parents
of Benjamin and Joseph Smith, manufacturers, of
Nelson, lived. On the opposite side was the dandy shop
for hand-loom weavers, with the old dye-works on the
left. Opposite again, was a nice house with a garden,
where Mr. Myers, a retired painter, lived; then a pretty
cottage in a garden. Here lived Miss Barbara and her
sister, two maiden ladies who knitted stockings and
gloves for the young folks of Colne. There are no hand-
knitted stockings nowadays. Then there were no idle
hands, for when a woman or girl went out to tea she
took her knitting with her and sat and chatted and
worked with her needles afterwards. Well, those old
ladies were very much respected and sought after. After
their cottage, there was nothing but green fields until
we reached Park Hill, then no more houses until Langroyd Farm, and the cottage in the fold, with its
beautiful garden of roses and honeysuckle climbing over
its walls. Here Christopher Edmondson and his wife,
Maria, had come to live and end their days after a life
of toil, amidst the peace and beauty of the fields
around. This was in the year 1855.

CHAPTER XII.

LANGROYD.

And gilded heels on dainty feet,
Have tripped at Langroyd's balls;
And voices long since hushed and still
Have sung within those walls;
Since first it rose up, fair and bright,
Upon that summer morn,
Amidst its sheltering trees, and saw,
Across the waving corn,
The bright sun cast his golden beams
Where Pendle Hill is piled,
And the Calder coil through hills and dales,
And many a rugged wild,
Flows on, through towns and villages,
Rippling, wild and free,
And flings its splashing, dashing self
Into the ruthless sea.

Changes have come to other halls,
But o'er the earth's green breast,
It still could see its coat of green
In sunlight glory drest.
Whilst, now rising and now falling,
O'er the trees and dusky dells,
In those far off days of glory
Rang Colunio's lovely bells.

How can I approach Langroyd without remembering
the many happy days I have spent there? There are
days in one's life that impress themselves upon the
memory, never to be forgotten. And I shall remember
the day I was shown the rooms at Langroyd to the
end. It impressed me as a girl quite as much as Chats-
worth did in later years. Now about the year 1852
Mrs. Carr called upon my sister Mary, who was a
milliner and straw bonnet maker, and in her own sweet
way ordered hats for herself and the children, who were
going into Rippondale to see Grandmamma Binns. The
things were sent home, and Mrs. Carr expressed her
delight and approval at the care and taste displayed in

them, and my sister was asked to call. She did so many times, doing a little plain sewing for Mrs. Carr, and even staying at Langroyd along with the cook and John Medlar, the man servant, when Mrs. Carr was away from home and had taken Sarah Bilsborough, the nurse-housemaid, with her to look after the children. It was on Mrs. Carr's return that I called with a parcel for my sister, and was shown through the house, which was splendid. Little did I think that summer morning that I should live there for over two years and remember it to the end of my days. There were the red room, the green room, and the brown room, and the beautiful drawing room, with its lovely needlework chairs and settees, was more than I could explain to my mother when I got home and told her of all the wonders I had seen. My mother laughed and said, "It's like being there to hear our Jane talk."

I lived two years at Langroyd, as nursemaid to Mrs. Carr, before the present owner, Mr. Edward Carr, was born, and never was there a more considerate or kinder mistress. She treated her servants as friends. Sometimes on a beautiful afternoon I would take the children out for a walk, and from the drive would glance back and see her sweet face smiling at me from the window over the porch. Another day I helped her to arrange her wardrobe, and she showed me her wedding dress, a beautiful flowered silk that had cost a hundred guineas. Ah, those were happy years, with so kind a mistress. I simply adored her; and is it any wonder that during the long toilsome years that were to follow, the marrying, and the bringing up of my own children, the loss of my husband, and the loss of old friends as the years rolled on, is it any wonder that I often thought of the past in my quiet moments, and of the peace and happiness of my days at Langroyd House? I remember my first day at Langroyd as though it were yesterday. It was sharp, frosty weather, in March. Mrs. Thornton, the nurse, was still there, but left the day after I arrived. Miss Ann Binns, Mrs. Carr's sister, was superintending the household. The routine was simple and regular on the first morning. John Medlar called the cook at 6-30; then he called the housemaid and me, and told me what I was to do before the children got up. There were two, James and Emily, to be washed and dressed by 8-30, breakfast in the nursery and the kitchen over by 9 o'clock, as Mr. Carr left for his office at that hour. I was not experienced enough to nurse the new baby, but I took the two elder ones out for a walk, accompanied by Miss Binns. This we did every morning, weather permitting. As I said before, the weather was cold and frosty, and for the first time I saw the reservoir frozen over. It seemed all very quiet and peaceful to me as I stood there, with the children's hands in mine, and Miss Binns beside me, looking round. For this was country indeed, after life in Colne.

It was shortly after I went to Langroyd that the new wing was built, by Whitehead and Holland, of Nelson. There was standing then a beautiful old place in the grounds, called The Garden House. There were stone steps outside, leading to the top room. The room underneath was called the tool room. It had small, leaded, diamond-shaped windows, and was covered with ivy and creepers. It was pulled down during the alterations. All the water was brought by John Medlar, except rain water, which was caught in a large stone trough in the yard, and used for washing clothes, etc. There was a new arrangement when I was there. John Medlar filled a cistern at the top of the house every morning, and we thought it grand when we could draw it through the taps, upstairs and down, and was a great saving of labour; except for John, who used to growl about the water we used, and, truth to tell, he had plenty to do, with three cows to milk, the pony and the garden to look after, shoes and knives to clean, etc. But every Englishman must have his grumble. It is their privilege, you know, and John was a good servant, and stayed many years. My life has been a series of ups and downs, so I must tell you of another tumble. John used to take the children out for a ride on the pony, each in a little basket slung over its back. One day when they came back, I said to John, "Let me have a ride." "Come on, then," said he. So he lifted the chair off, as he called it, put on a side saddle, and lifted me on, and off I went round and round the field, when suddenly something began to slip, and in a moment over I went. There was some mud near at hand, and as the song says:

> I was in it,
> Fairly in it,
> I went head first in that mud,
> And there I fairly stuck.

I'll never forget how John laughed, and the cook as well, who had been watching me. "Tha'll nooan want to ride ageean," she said. "Oh, won't I," said I, and went to get washed. The Carrs entertained a little now and again. A notable event during my stay was a dinner, given to His Honour Judge Addison. Amongst the guests were Mr. Waddington Hartley, Mr. Birdsworth, from Lytham, a cousin of Mr. Carr; Mr. George Carr, Dr. Ayre, and a few others. It was a bachelors' dinner, except for the presence of Mrs. Carr, who did the honours gracefully and sweetly, as was her wont, and her sister, Miss Binns. I helped Sarah Bilsborough to wait at table, while John Medlar was in the room, dressed in his best livery. After dinner, the children were dressed and presented to the visitors. I remember the table, how beautiful it looked, with its flowers, its cut glass and gleaming silver. It was the first beautifully-arranged table I had seen, and I never forgot it. They did not keep late hours at Langroyd in those days. 10-30 was the time for locking up. A large dog, called Nell, was brought in and chained to the kitchen dresser, with a cushion for its bed, and in a few moments all was quiet for the night.

CHAPTER XII.

I remember one afternoon Mrs. Carr came to the nursery and told us to get ready and she would take us to the Cloth Hall to see some very wonderful marion-

ettes. They were only dolls, you know, similar to those
shown by the ventriloquists of to-day, but more wonderful. They acted on a miniature stage, with movements
so life-like you would have thought them living beings.
On this occasion they played "The Babes in the Wood,"
and James and Emily, Mrs. Carr's two children, cried
when the birds covered the babes with leaves; but burst
into laughter when an old man and woman came on,
dressed like street singers, and sang,

Oh, cruel was the captain,
And bitter was the day,
When they took those sweet babes
And sent them far away.

Then the old woman turned to the old man and cried,
"Chorus, Tommy," and he in a tinny voice sang:
Oh, to-ral o-ral i-dow
To-ral-o-ral-ay.

This amused the children very much, and us, too, for
that matter, for often during the next few months
Emily would act the marionettes and say to James,
"Chorus, Tommy," and they would sing the choruses
again, to Mrs. Carr's great amusement.

Sometimes in our walks up Red-lane we would call on
Mrs. Metcalfe, who was very fond of the children. Her
son, Hartley Metcalfe, was a butcher in Colne, and
supplied the house with meat. John, another son,
farmed for his mother. Mrs. Carr sometimes accompanied us, and told me stories of her own girlhood, and
pointed out to me the hills around, for Malham Rocks
could be seen on a fine clear day. Another time, Mr.
Carr had business at Barnoldswick, so we went with the
children a drive to White Moor. We called on Mrs.
Rushworth, and asked if we could have a boat out on
the reservoir. She said her husband was away on the
moors with his gun, but she would take us, and she did.
Oh, it was grand to see this splendid type of young
English womanhood bend to the oars as gracefully as a
college athlete, and send the boat flying over the water.

England need not fear for her future when there are such mothers of her sons as this. How often I have thought of her since, and as I write I can see her again, her round, red arms bare to the shoulder, gripping the oars; her eyes sparkling, and an amused smile on her red lips as we gripped the sides of the boat. I did not know it then, but that day I was introduced for the first time into my future husband's family, for my husband, Joseph Cryer, was nephew to Joshua Rushworth, whose sister married Mr. John Cryer, of Holt Head Farm, near Burnley. But to return to Langroyd and its pleasant home life. When the new wing was finished we all had our portraits taken in front of the house. Mr. Carr was away, but Mr. George Carr, Mrs. Carr, and the children were taken walking down the front path. John and I, cook and Sarah, stood in the background. In the following summer, when we went to Mr. Birdsworth's, at Lytham, to stay, they had one of the groups in the drawing room.

But the time came when my happy days at Langroyd were drawing to a close, and Ellen Anderson, the cook, called me to her and said, "Now, let me tell thee, Jane, thou hast always been a good girl, for thou hast never given me a back answer since thou came." Dear old Ellen Anderson, so kind and considerate to everyone. She was afterwards housekeeper to Mr. Frank Richmond, of Colne, and stayed many years. Then my dear mistress called me up into her own little room over the porch, where she used to sit and wait for the master coming home, and where, sometimes, when the children were put to bed, she would have me in to sit with her and keep her company. She took my hand in her own kind, caressing way, and said, "Good bye, Jane. Refer anyone to me. I will always speak for you; but come and see me again." And so I left Langroyd, as the sun was setting in the west and gilding the old place and its surroundings in a crimson glory. Darkness fell as I entered Colne, and for days it seemed to me as if I'd left all sunshine, all brightness, and all happiness behind. The years rolled on, and I was in London when the dear old "Colne and Nelson Times" came and told

me of her death. The room faded from my sight. I
was a girl again in a country lane. How sweet, how
fresh, how beautiful the day was! There must be wild
roses growing somewhere in the hedges, for I can smell
their fragrance. Then I was again in that room over
the porch and my mistress was saying, "Good bye,
Jane." How sweet it was and how real! Ah, me! For
in a moment all the sad weary years had rolled away,
and I was holding the children by the hand and wandering up Red Lane, listening to their prattle as I went.
There was a rustle as the paper fell from my knees to
the floor. I picked it up, and as I did so up to my
window came the eternal roar of London. The dream
vanished, and the reality was the paper I held in my
hand with its message of death. That night these lines
were penned, "in memoriam" of Mrs. Carr, of Langroyd,
at the request of Jane Ward, a former nursemaid:

Ah, me, I remember well the time
And far away I see
Through all the dusk of the long ago
Thy kindly smile to me.
I silently hold the children's hands,
I listen, 'tis they who talk;
I see fair Colne on the distant hill,
I dream on the garden walk.
I pass the shrubbery at the gate,
I wander up Red Lane,
But the mistress and friend of the long ago
I ne'er shall see again.
Years have gone by since those old sweet days,
The days of thy life's young spring,
When thy children fair around thee were
The centre of everything.
With a loving smile and a last good-night,
Thou knelt thee down to pray.
I hear thy voice to Him above,
He was thy guide, thy stay.
Oh, mistress and friend, in the light of the sun,
Thou art at rest with the beautiful one.
Thinking alone, as the midnight chimes,
In fancy I see thee still,

Langroyd Hall was built in 1605 by John Hartley; in later years it was home to the Carr family, one of whom, Edward, a solicitor, was twice mayor of Colne. His brother James was the author of 'The Annals of Colne'. It was while Edward was in residence that General William Booth, founder of the Salvation Army, stayed at the hall for a week. In the following years the hall was used as a maternity home during the 1940s and later as a public house.

Langroyd about 1880. The house in the centre was Myers House, whose outbuildings were removed when North Valley Road was opened up.

Will E. Halliwell,

"THERMOS" and
"ISOLA" FLASKS
from 3/6 ;
And all Novelties of Merit.

WATCHES,
JEWELLERY,
SPECTACLES.

Market St., Colne.

"Colne & Nelson Times,"

ESTABLISHED 1874.

1d.	EVERY FRIDAY MORNING.	1d.

*Only Newspaper Printed and Published
in Colne.*

With many a kindly word and smile
To friends on old Colne hill;
Helping the poor with a bounteous hand,
For deep in that heart of thine,
The poor had a friend that could understand,
And pity had found a shrine.
Oh, mistress and friend, that I used to know,
We yet shall meet in the afterglow.
Ah, me! I remember the dear old friends,
I dream in the summer haze,
I see my mistress at the porch,
And phantoms of other days,
Gather round the fire, while without,
The darkening fields along,
Is borne upon the evening air,
The strains of an olden song.
But the lights are out that lit the feast,
And friends have vanished and music ceased.
I remember the days, the old sweet days,
When the children and I would go,
Where the shadows lay cool, and the calves were feeding.
Wandering to and fro;
When the air from the hills blew keen and sweet,
And no thought that the fates could sever,
How sweet 't was to roam in the noontide heat,
And dream it would last for ever.
But borne on the air is a funeral bell.
Mistress and friend, farewell! farewell!

CHAPTER XIV.

It is a long time since the first Old Folks' Tea-party
was held in the Cloth Hall. I remember a gentleman
calling to see my grandmother when she was a long
way over 70 years of age. She lived to be 85. She
said she would be glad to go, but when she heard it was
free entertainment and tea she was very indignant and
refused to go, saying she would have nothing on charity
as she had always paid her way, thank God. But when
it was explained that it was a sort of gathering together

E

of old friends, men and women, just to see how many old people there were, she consented, "if Jane would take her and call for her when it was over." So, of course, Jane had to go. Then it became the sole topic of conversation until the eventful day arrived. She wondered if so-and-so would be there, and would they know her? Had she altered much? Her hair was not so very grey, was it? And, thank goodness, it was not as thin as Mrs. So-and-So's; she had hardly any, and so on, until my mother did not know what she was doing half her time, while my brothers laughed at her natural anxiety to look her best. So we went to the Cloth Hall, and when my grandmother walked into the room where the old people were, three or four of them came to us and said, "Why, its Jenny Edmondson." Then they shook hands and kissed each other, and laughed just like happy children, and got her by the hand, saying "Come and sit thee down. Aye, Aw am glad to see thee." Then they cried for joy at the meetings of old friends whom they had not seen for years. My grandmother talked of this first Old Folks' Tea Party for days. She had seen Jack Halstead, whose brother had been a farm servant, and one day, at hay-making time, had had a row with his master, and swore, in a drunken temper, that he hoped if ever he lifted a spade in his master's service again the Lord would strike him dead. The next morning, after sleeping the drink off, one of his friends talked him over and prevailed on him to start work and let byegones be byegones. He went to the field, picked up a spade, struck the earth two or three times, then cuddled down on to the grass and died. Then she had seen Sarah Ancross, who was 69, and told my grandmother that she had buried three husbands and was looking out for a fourth. Then there was Mary Varley, whose husband, Jack Varley, was the hero of a rather startling adventure. He was fond of the cup that cheers and does inebriate, and usually arrived home

> So early in the morning,
> So early in the morning,
> So early in the morning,
> Before the break of day.

Colne Parish Church (before its restoration).

You must remember I am writing of a time many years before Mr. Gladstone's Early Closing Bill came into force, when the "pubs." kept open until 2 o'clock sometimes, then, closing their doors for an hour, opened again at 3 or 4 o'clock, and very often the customers were not turned out, but stayed in drinking. Well, one night, or rather, morning, Jack Varley did not arrive home as usual, and Mary, feeling anxious, went out in search of him, making her way straight to the White Horse, opposite the church. She enquired if he was there? No, he had gone an hour ago. "Was he drunk?" asked Mary. "Well," said the landlord drily, "he'd had a drop." So off set Mary again in her search for her lord, three of the customers volunteering to go with her, fearing something might have happened to him. Passing the church railings they were startled by hearing a dismal groan come from amongst the tombstones. Mary screamed and scuttled into the roadway. They listened, then came the sound of snoring. Borrowing a lantern from the White Horse, they got into the churchyard, and, after a search, came upon an open grave, and lying in the bottom was Jack Varley, sound asleep. They prodded him with the handle of a long rake until he awoke, when one of the party, tying a white handkerchief over his head and wrapping Mary's white shawl around him, gave Jack a final prod to rouse him, and, leaning over the grave, cried in a sepulchral voice, "What are you doing in my grave at 3 o'clock in the morning?" Jack rose up, looked a bit scared, and then cried, "What the ——— are you doing out of your grave at 3 o'clock in the morning?"

"And who else does ta think was there, Marget?" said my grandmother. "Aye, I don't know," said my mother. "Nancy Baldwin. Oh, and she does look old. Jack's dead; lived just ten years after t' wedding. One lass is married an' lives i' Burnley. and the only lad they had 'listed and died in India. Aye, 'oo fair cried when 'oo saw me, because I was at her wedding and 'oo came to mine, and we couldn't help but think of the past. Oh, Aw have enjoyed mysel. Aye, Aw'm glad Aw went," she said. Then I told my mother about standing at the door of the room and waiting to take my grandmother home, and about the fiddlers beginning to play:

Oh, dear, what can the matter be,
Oh, dear, what can the matter be,
Oh, dear, what can the matter be,
Johnnie's so long at the fair?
He promised to buy me a bunch of blue ribbon,
He promised to buy me a bunch of blue ribbon,
He promised to buy me a bunch of blue ribbon,
To tie up my bonny brown hair.

"To tie up my bonny brown hair," sang the old folks, forgetting their troubles in the joy of the moment, while their feet kept time to the music, which grew faster and faster. Then one old dame would jerk on to her feet, and another, gaining confidence, would follow suit. Then a jolly-faced old man of 70 laughed, and, laying down his stick, took his partner into the middle of the room, and they were soon all dancing the old country dances, as happy as children. And why shouldn't they? Why shouldn't age be as happy as youth? Aye, and happier, if life has been well spent. For age knows that rest is near at hand, and youth, with all its vague dreams of the future, is past. This was the first Old Folks' Tea-party. I saw it as a child, and if God spares me until the next, I will be there, and maybe some other girl may stand where I stood, and in the dim future, when age has come to her, as it comes to us all, she, too, may write her "Memories of Colne," as I am doing.

For lives of great men all remind us,
We can make our lives sublime;
And, departing, leave behind us
Footprints on the sands of time.

Here, too, in the Cloth Hall, 60 years ago, the public balls were held. And what grand assemblies they were! Here and there would be seen the red coats of the officers (for Colne was a garrison town) showing in marked contrast to the white dresses of the ladies, who wore their hair in curls tied with pink ribbon, and tripped through the dances in sandal slippers. But come with me, and I will show it to you. A crowd of people, smiles on every lip, lights flashing, the dreamy strains of a waltz floats out on the night air, and through the doors pass all that are bravest and best of the sons and daughters of Old Colne. Its leading tradesmen; pretty girls, accompanied by their best young men; lawyers' clerks and shopmen jostle their way into the great room. It is eleven of the clock as we enter, and in the chaos of noise and colour it is difficult to recognise anyone. But wait. That handsome young man leading the girl to a seat is Leonard Henderson. See, he is introducing her brother to Miss Hillary. What beautiful hair, you say! Yes, it is like moonlight on a summer sea. But look round the room. Everywhere there are smiles, the flash of bright eyes, the gleam of white teeth and polished shoulders. That is Miss Jackson, from the Fleece Inn, talking to young Petty. The Misses Goddard, dancing with Mr. Butler and young Haighton. And there is Miss Hudson, with her merry laugh. There is pretty Miss Baldwin, handsome Fanny Dobson, and Alice Lomas talking to Jim Medley; and look, there are Tom Hey and Nancy Strickland off together. Can't they dance? And Tom Ward and Margaret Clitheroe talking to Mary Asquith and Miss Schofield. Those girls who have just passed us are the Misses Veevers; and that is Margaret Clegg talking to Mrs. Stuttard. Oh, what a splendid sight it was; the gleam and glitter of the lights, the rustle of the dresses, the low, sweet music, the flowers, the perfume, the colours—green, mauve, yellow, and blue—the voices, the low, sweet laughter, the glances from bright eyes, the slender, graceful girls, the bright-faced handsome lads. Where are you all to-day? Oh, the Cloth Hall on a ball night 60 years ago was a very rosebud garden of youth and Colne maidenhood.

Waterside, one of the oldest parts of Colne, remained throughout the centuries a textile producing area and also produced some of Colne's notable figures. Sir Wiliam Pickles Hartley, Peter Birtwistle, Edmondson Spencer, Tom Shaw and Luther Greenwood, all men of energy and determination, were born in Waterside. On the left of the picture was Samuel Hartley, grocer, whose shop was taken over by Hettie Wilde in 1908.

Higgin House was built in the 1770s and was once the home of Dr A A Dickey, resident surgeon at the Cottage Hospital.

J. H. GREENWOOD,

REMBRANDT ART STUDIO,

North Valley Road, COLNE

(Within 3 minutes' walk of Station and Electric Cars.)

HIGH-CLASS PHOTOGRAPHY
AT MODERATE PRICES.

Enlargements by all Processes.   Water-Colour Miniatures
in all the Latest Shapes.

Child Portraiture a Speciality.

Photographs taken Day or Night.
Special Electric Installation for Night Work.

Tel. 299.   *When possible, appointments should be made.*

CHAPTER XV.

I remember when the old Cloth Hall was used as a barracks by the soldiers, and I remember them marching to church every Sunday morning. They used to sit near the christening font under the gallery on the left of the porch. My brothers used to tell a rather amusing story of the meeting of a local preacher and one of those "boys in red." The soldier laddie had dined not wisely but too well, and our saintly friend met him when he was toddling home,

> So early in the morning,
> So early in the morning,
> So early in the morning,
> Before the break of day.

"Where are you going, brother?" said the preacher, trying to steady our country's brave defender up against the wall. "To the barracks, of co-course," hiccoughed the lad, "Where are ta going?" "I," said the preacher, clasping his hands and gazing up to the midnight sky, "I am going to heaven." "Oh ar ta," said the soldier. "Then all I can say is, tha art a —— sight farther away fra thy barracks than I am. Ta, ta." It was a bright scene, and yet a saddening one when they left Colne for good. I think all Colne must have turned out to watch them go. They formed up in line outside the barracks. The drums sounded and the bands commenced to play "The girl I left behind me," and to that lilting music they marched through the streets to the station, the women running at their sides and some throwing their arms around the lads' necks and kissing them as they went. How some of the girls did cry! It was pitiful. "Oh, why are you going away," cried a bright-faced girl? "Well, you see," said the Sergeant, "You are all so good there is nothing for us to do, but we will come again if you want us." So the soldiers went out of the life of Colne, and, putting sentiment aside, Colne was the better for it.

I think of all the strange costumes ever adopted by my own sex the bloomer costume was the most ridiculous, and yet even that was worn in Colne streets 60 years ago. There stood on Colne Field, then, an old stone building, in use as a school. Well, a new schoolmaster and mistress were expected, and, judge of our surprise, when she did come, she made her appearance in bloomers. They were nothing more nor less than men's trousers with the addition of a frill round the bottom that hung over the boot tops. But over the trousers she wore a skirt reaching to the knees. The whole rig-out was made of a dark brown material, and you can just imagine how the good folks of Colne turned out to see the two of them go back from the school to their home in the row of houses in Albert-road below the Wesleyan Chapel, called William Asquith Houses. During their stay in Colne, which was not long, they were followed everywhere by gangs of children, and were a source of much laughter and jokes among the good wives of the old town, who, I know, tried their husband's Sunday suits on when their lords were out, just to see how they looked in bloomers. But, of course, no Colne wife was brave enough to venture out in them. "Well," my mother cried, raising her hands in horror the first time she saw this lady, "the brazen-faced hussy."

Another well-known character in Colne 60 years ago was Tommy Driver, who had a shop in Clayton Street. He was a well known Wesleyan, and established the first Insurance Club in Colne, which he called "A death club." When anyone died who was in Tommy Driver's death club, Tommy attended the funeral himself in person as chief mourner, and walked at the head of the procession, carrying a badge and a long black stick decorated at the top with a bunch of black ribbon. Previous to Tommy Driver's death club, it was the custom for every friend who called upon a bereaved family to drop a shilling into the hand of the nearest relative of the dead person, who usually sat at the head of the coffin and lifted the cover from the face of the dead for the friend to take one last look thereon. This was one of the ways that the poor had of helping the poor,

JOHN HORSFIELD

BOOT
MAKER,

"K" Boots
fitted accurately
from stock, in
perfected styles
and shapes.

AGENCY for
"K"
BOOTS.

16, ALBERT ROAD,
COLNE.

THOMAS LANCASTER,

COMPLETE HOUSE FURNISHER,
SKELTON STREET, COLNE.

Coffins Made.
FUNERALS FURNISHED THROUGHOUT.

**Best Prices given for Second-hand Furniture in Exchange
for New.**
Agent for the "Shetlun" Bedding.

Sound Tailoring

AND IMITATION.

You get the FORMER at

H. J. BOGUE'S

ALBERT ROAD,

COLNE.

Beautify the surroundings of your Home by giving your Garden a consideration. If you possess a Garden, no matter where you live, if you will only come to us, we will advise you what to plant to thrive well and suit your purpose. We have Trees, Shrubs, and Hardy Roots, suitable for growing in the town or country.
Come and see them growing.

B. SMITH & SON,
Nurserymen & Landscape Gardeners,
ROSEHILL NURSERY, HAVERHOLT,
COLNE.
Shop: 62a, Albert Rd.

Residence: Rosehill.

We specialise in **ROSES.** We have also, in great variety, ORNAMENTAL TREES AND SHRUBS, FOREST AND FRUIT TREES, HARDY ROOTS, HERBACEOUS AND ALPINE PLANTS, GREENHOUSE PLANTS for Sale or Hire, SEED, BULBS, Sundries, in fact everything for the Garden.

Old Colne Hall.

for before the days of cheap insurance it would have gone
hard with some if one had not lent the other a helping
hand.

There stood then, out in the fields, some old cottages,
called by old Colners, The Castle. I do not know why,
for anything more unlike a castle you cannot imagine.
Well, the daughter of one of the cottagers died, and my
mother, who baked the funeral bread and cakes, sent me
with it in a basket, and gave me the usual shilling.
When I got ·to the cottage, Tommy Driver was ·just
finishing a prayer to the company, and when we came
outside he gave out a hymn. The coffin of the girl was
lifted on to the shoulders of four lads, and covered with
flowers. After the coffin came her companions, in
white, and carrying white flowers in their hands. Then
slowly over the fields we went towards Colne, raising our
voices in a hymn of praise to Him Who is the Father of
us all. The sun poured down in a blaze of splendour
that summer afternoon, as slowly and solemnly we neared
the Old Church, the Church that has seen so many
happy brides, carrying with us the bride of death. In
thinking that, perchance our hymns did not fall upon
dull ears, and it may be that she was happier than any
earthly bride. For all around summer smiled in her
splendour, and the silence of the church as we entered
it spoke of God, and rest, and peace profound.

Now, dear old friends, I will tell you of my own
wedding at the Old Church, and then,

Farewell.
A word which must be and hath been,
A word which makes us linger,
Yet, Farewell,
You who have traced the pilgrim to this scene,
Which is the last.

For my "Memories of Colne" are almost at an end.
I need not tell you what a pleasure it has been to me
to be with you all again, for age, you know, lives in the
past. And it is sweet to remember the old days, for

I hear your well-loved voices, friends,
O'er all the years gone by ;
Oh, how my heart reioices, friends,
But oh, I want to cry.

Well, I remember the night well that my future
husband asked me to be his wife, because when I got
home I knelt down and prayed to God to make me a
good wife; and I was so happy. Why, I wouldn't have
changed places with Queen Victoria. So the next day
I consulted my mother, who was very pleased, for she
liked my future husband, who was a teacher under Mr.
Grant, at St. Peter's School, Burnley. My lover wanted
to be married by special licence, but my mother said,
"Nay, the owd fashioned askings at church were best."
So asked I was. Besides, as my mother said, "We
could do with the money, and a licence cost a lot."
Joe Cryer, my future husband, had saved £20, and I
had £5. Not much to begin housekeeping on, you
think. Well, no, it was not, but some have much less.
I had been waitress at Cranwood House for three years,
and it was my sister Mary who taught me to save and
be careful, otherwise I should not have had a penny.
My wedding dress of brown and white striped silk was
bought. My sister's dress was of blue and white silk,
and the night before my wedding day, when all in our
house at Spring Lane top were asleep, except my mother
and I, I went out and cleaned and stoned the front door
step by the light of the moon, so that all should be
bright and ready the following day. What a morning
that was, when we got to church and we stood near the
altar ! I saw quite a crowd of friends had secured places
to watch us, while a lot more were outside, waiting to
give us a send-off. I looked at our pew, where I had sat
Sunday after Sunday since childhood. Then I heard
Mr. Owen's voice, and soon it was all over. "Oh, lass,"
said an old friend of my mother's, "tha's teed a knot
with thy tongue thoul't never loise with thy teeth."

CHAPTER XVI.

How the little lads and lasses ran by the side of our carriages when we left the church gates, and what a chattering and hugging and kissing there was when we got home! My mother stood there with tears in her eyes. I am sure she saw visions of her own wedding day years and years ago, and my girl friends laughed and wondered when their own wedding would fall due. And the breakfast! What a beautiful spread! Well, it simply gave you an appetite to look at it, besides a grand wedding cake and one to take away with us to our new home. My mother had made cakes of every description. Well, it was over at last, and the table wanted clearing. My word, the willing helpers we had! All my girl friends wanted to wash up and clean the cups and saucers, although they had their best Sunday clothes on; and before long they were running here, there and everywhere, colliding with each other and putting the articles into the wrong places, and laughing gaily at their exploits. Then we shook hands all round, kissed those we were entitled to kiss, and some we had never kissed before, while my mother stood looking at me with tears in her eyes, and her hands trembling slightly as she leant on a chair. I went over and kissed her. Then we donned our hats, and coats and gloves and sallied outside, where four carriages awaited us. We drove to Skipton and had dinner at the Brick Hall, ordered beforehand. The weather, which in the morning was fine and cold (it was December), in the afternoon became cloudy and overcast. Then it came down "cats and dogs," as the saying is. It thundered and lightninged when we reached Thornton, so we put up at the Broughton Arms and waited until the rain ceased. It was fine for our drive home. We had a late tea with Mr. and Mrs. Griffiths, late of the Talbot Hotel, Burnley.

The best man at our wedding was Mr. Tom Bland, Burnley, and my bridesmaid my sister Mary. The guests included: Mr. Wilkinson (Daneshouse), and Miss Blackburn, Miss Alice Cryer (my husband's sister), Mr.

Colne Market Cross (from a Drawing).

John Rushworth (cousin), Mr. George Bulcock and Miss E. Asquith (Colne Lane), Mr. and Mrs. Edwin Griffiths (Iron Foundry, Burnley), Mr. Jack Pilkington (Goole), my brothers Jonathan and Edmondson (who would not say he would come until the very last, and it was only when he had upset my mother with his temper that he went and dressed himself and came amongst us). There was also a Mrs. Ord, from Primet Bridge, a great friend of my mother, and a great comfort to her after I had left home.

Compared with the long lists of wedding presents one sees in large type in the papers to-day, mine were not so numerous or grand. A copper kettle, from Mr. Elijah Helm; a step-ladder chair, a pair of brass candle-sticks, a salt box, for luck, from the cook at Langroyd; a set of china cups and saucers, from the Misses Greenwood, Crow-wood House; also a fine goose to be sent to old Mrs. Cryer, of Duckpits Farm, for our use; a turkey, from cousin Jack Rushworth, Stacksteads Farm: and a large piece of corned beef (not the American production, that was unknown), a pickled tongue and plum pudding, from Mr. Pilkington, of Goole; and an invitation to spend Christmas there. Such were my presents. What amusement it would create if such a list was appended to a marriage notice to-day! Oh, but things were different 50 or 60 years ago. Now I will tell you how it was that I thought of the "Memories of Colne." You know how the mind wanders over the past in our quiet moments. So on my birthday, four years ago, in 1906, I was sitting alone in my room, dreaming of old scenes and vanished friends, when I took up a book and idly jotted down a few notes about the things I remembered in my life. My son, Willie Cryer, came in and wished me many happy returns of the day. "What are you doing, mother?" he asked. "Look," I said, handing him the book. "Very good," he said, "but what good will it do you?" "Well, I don't know," I answered, "but I might write a little more some day." That was the beginning. Now the son who came in so short a time ago, apparently in full health, is gone to join the father who died 20 years ago. My brothers and sisters are all gone, too. Mary, my sister, was a widow when she died, and left three children. I took them and brought them up at Rosegrove. Then I kept the Mill-stone Inn, 25, St. James's-street, Burnley, for ten years, under the Old Brewery. Then for three years I kept a public-house in London. Returning to Burnley, I opened the Prince's Restaurant, 4, St. James'-street, staying at that address 11 years. The same business I transferred to my present address; here, in my quiet moments, I look back over a long life. A happy life, too, it has been, thank God. For He has given me health and strength to fight its battles and enjoy its pleasures. Not the least has been jotting down these "Memories" for you, which have brought me into touch once more with many dear old friends. I will quote a couple of letters I have received from two old Colners, who still look back with love to the days of their youth in the "Town upon the Hill" : —

"Sheffield, July 2nd, 1910. — Dear Madam, — My wife has asked me to write you to say how pleased she has been in reading your 'Memories of Colne,' in the 'Colne and Nelson Times.' She is a native of Colne, and lived next door but one to you at Spring Lane top, and she has a small brooch you gave her when you were girls together. It is 44 years since I went to Colne, and 36 years since we were married at Nelson Wesleyan Chapel, and 35½ years since we came to Sheffield. Betsy, at Mrs. Blackburn's, used to be my landlady, and although I did not know Mrs. B., I knew one who was once her scholar, Miss Rubina Hartley. I am sure your 'Memories' are proving very entertaining to all old Colners, and I congratulate you on the wonderful memory you must have. I remember Edmondson Ward very well. My wife was Elizabeth Foulds, and she was about 11 years of age when you gave her the brooch. She is now 64½. With best wishes from my wife and myself, yours sincerely, C. W. Fryer."

The next is from Leeds. "My dear old friend, — I am very delighted to read your 'Memories' of dear old Colne 60 years ago. I have the paper sent to me by the late Mrs. Tatham's youngest daughter, Mrs. Stuttard, of Alkincoates Road, Colne, and am quite charmed with all you say, and, although I was brought to Leeds by my beloved parents when very young indeed, I do remember a good deal about my birth place, and enjoy reading your 'Memories' most of all. Come and see me if ever you are in our city. Accept my love and best wishes.— Believe me, your attached old friend, Pattie Pickard."

This is the Martha Hudson I have mentioned in my "Memories." So there are others who love to dream in the evening of their days of the happy years gone by, but I hope to see them both once again.

Then, after the lapse of years we'll meet,
And sit for a while together,
Recrossing the dim and vanished years,
In the best and worst of weather.

Once more, come with me back to the Old Church, the church where we worshipped as children, and where we stood as happy, careless girls, and watched the dead and gone ladies of a vanished day sweep up that aisle in their flashing silks and satins. And there I will leave you, for where better could I leave you than at the altar of God and near the grave of my dear father and mother?

Old home, upon Old Colne hillside,
Farewell, it is the eventide.

[The End.]

J. W. MIDGLEY,

✠

ESTABLISHED 1885.

Ladies' and Gents'

Tailor.

TELEPHONE 5x1.

✠

CHURCH STREET, COLNE.

Parkinsons'
BAKING POWDER

Is Absolutely Pure and Reliable.

In a word, it is, like Parkinsons' Drugs,

THE VERY BEST OBTAINABLE.

PARKINSONS'

CUSTARD POWDER.

A Penny Packet makes a :: ::
Pint of DELICIOUS CUSTARD.

Try it with Stewed or Tinned Fruits.

Your Grocer sells both the above, and also

PARKINSONS' PURE DRUGS.